Communication

No. 302

WRITING SKILLS

Published
for
The National Examinations Board for Supervisory Studies
in conjunction with
The Northern Regional Management Centre

by
Pergamon Open Learning
a division of
Pergamon Press

Oxford · New York · Beijing · Frankfurt
São Paulo · Sydney · Tokyo · Toronto

U.K.	Pergamon Press plc, Headington Hill Hall, Oxford OX3 0BW, England
U.S.A.	Pergamon Press, Inc., Maxwell House, Fairview Park, Elmsford, New York 10523, U.S.A.
PEOPLE'S REPUBLIC OF CHINA	Pergamon Press, Room 4037, Quianmen Hotel, Beijing, People's Republic of China
FEDERAL REPUBLIC OF GERMANY	Pergamon Press GmbH, Hammerweg 6, D-6242 Kronberg, Federal Republic of Germany
BRAZIL	Pergamon Editora Ltda, Rua Eça de Queiros, 346, CEP 04011, Paraiso, São Paulo, Brazil
AUSTRALIA	Pergamon Press Australia Pty Ltd., P.O. Box 544, Potts Point, N.S.W. 2011, Australia
JAPAN	Pergamon Press, 5th Floor, Matsuoka Central Building, 1-7-1 Nishishinjuku, Shinjuku-Ku, Tokyo 160, Japan
CANADA	Pergamon Press Canada Ltd., Suite No. 271, 253 College Street, Toronto, Ontario, Canada M5T 1R5

First edition 1985

Reprinted 1987, 1989

British Library Cataloguing in Publication Data

Writing skills.—(Super series. Open learning for
supervisory management; no. 302)
1. English language—Business English
2. English language—Writing
I. National Examinations Board for Supervisory Studies
II. Northern Regional Management Centre
III. Series
808'.066651021   PE1115

ISBN 0-08-033963-8

This work was produced under an Open Tech contract with the Manpower Services Commission. The views expressed are those of the authors and do not necessarily reflect those of the MSC or any Government Department or the Publisher.

Project Manager: Pam Sear
Material Source: NRMC
Author: Diana Thomas
Editor: Harry V. Pardue
Illustrations: NEBSS

CONTENTS

PART F   UNIT REVIEW

INTRODUCTION TO THE SUPER SERIES

OPEN LEARNING

The Super Series has been designed as a text-and-tape presentation for those who prefer self-study or who cannot attend courses on a regular basis.

As an open learning student, you have the opportunity of making a selection of units from our list to match your own requirements and you can study them when and where you wish.

TUTORIAL SUPPORT

Each unit has been written in such a way that you can study on your own. Although the units are complete in themselves, in some cases they provide not only *knowledge* but the opportunity of developing *skills*. In order to gain these skills you will need to join with others working in small groups in a Support Centre approved by the National Examinations Board for Supervisory Studies (NEBSS).

These centres can also help with any queries that may arise from your study of the unit and offer facilities such as libraries, microcomputers and videos in addition to tutorial assistance both by telephone and in the Centre.

If you would like help in designing your own programme of study, take the FREE CONSULTATION voucher included with this unit to the OPEN LEARNING TUTOR at your nearest Support Centre. The tutor will also be able to give you details of the fees payable for the use of the Centre's facilities and for tutorial assistance.

STUDY NOTES

INTRODUCTION

This Unit of Study, like all those in the 'Super Series' is specially designed for studying on your own. This means that you can work at your own pace, and where and when you like. If you have a query, need help or want to join a group in order to develop skills as well as knowledge, your nearest NEBSS Support Centre can help you.

STUDY METHODS

Where. You can listen to the tape in the car or at home. You can read the workbook anywhere. But if you want to get the most from it you need to be able to concentrate without distractions like conversation, TV or children! You will also need somewhere to keep your workbook, papers and tape recorder together and in order.

When. This is entirely up to you. The writers who prepared the Units think that you will be able to complete them in about eight hours, though don't be dismayed if it takes longer than this as we all learn different things at different speeds. The best way, of course, is to plan in advance and to set aside a certain time on certain days in order to complete the Unit satisfactorily.

If the Unit forms a part of a training course, or you are working for a NEBSS Module Award and want to join a group, you may need to take these into account when you decide on your timetable.

Perhaps the best advice is not to be too ambitious but start *regular* periods of study — say an hour at a time. This will yield far better results than occasional long periods.

How. Listen to the first side of the tape and then read the workbook, section by section.

This has Activities and Self-Checks and your success in these will indicate how well you are doing. If you find that you are not doing very well, go back over the text and try again. It may be that you were in too much of a hurry.

Make notes in the workbook, or in a file if you want to discuss them with a tutor, of key points, because actually writing them down is a very useful way of helping to memorise them. If you keep your tape recorder handy you can record ideas or queries as they occur to you.

References to books, videos and films are also made in this workbook for those who want to study in greater depth. The Support Centre or your local library will be able to supply copies.

CONCENTRATE ON WHAT YOU ARE STUDYING, READ AND LISTEN UNTIL YOU HAVE GRASPED THE MATTER NOT JUST FOR AN HOUR OR TWO BUT SO THAT IT REMAINS WITH YOU. And if you can discuss the facts and ideas with other people this will develop your understanding and help to retain them in your mind.

HELP!   Help is available from

- Yourself. Go back and try again. Don't give up. If you don't understand or sometimes find it hard going, go back to it at the beginning of your next study period.

- Your family or friends. Even if they don't understand the subject the act of discussing it sometimes clarifies the point in your mind.

- Your training staff at work.

- The Support Centre, by phone or a visit (but phone for an appointment on your first visit).

UNIT OBJECTIVES

Most of us don't like having to write things down but, as a supervisor, you are almost bound to have to put pen to paper sometimes — whether it is a routine entry in the shift log or a special one-off report on work in your section, a brief telex or a long and difficult letter.

Whatever it is we have to write we each develop a characteristic style of writing and our aims should be to make that style as clear, brief and easy to understand as possible — for our own satisfaction and for the reader's sake.

IN THIS UNIT WE WILL:

● identify when we need to write;

● examine ways of developing a clear, simple style;

● examine ways of organising what we want to say.

AUDIO TAPE
Side 1

Before you continue through the unit, you should listen to Side 1 of the audio tape that accompanies the unit. You will find it useful if you refer to the unit objectives shown below whilst you listen to the tape. You may wish to make the objectives clearer to yourself by making a note or two on the page as you listen.

OBJECTIVES

When you have completed this unit you will be BETTER ABLE to:

● identify the SITUATIONS in which you need to write things down;

● make your writing SIMPLE, DIRECT and ACTIVE;

● vary the STRUCTURE of your writing to increase the reading INTEREST;

● organise your writing to make UNDERSTANDING EASIER and RESPONSE MORE LIKELY.

PART A   WHEN TO WRITE

1.   Introduction

How much writing we have to do varies from one job to another. Some supervisors and their workteams may spend several hours a day at a desk writing their own letters, reports, telexes. Others may just have to adapt standard communications to meet the particular case they are dealing with and some may keep their writing to a minimum and not have to do more than occasionally complete standard forms.

But, if you are a supervisor, then you are responsible for communicating with your workteam and communicating what is happening in your work area to people outside it. And to do this effectively, you may need to write something down rather than talking.

It's not that writing in itself is in any way 'better' than talking. They are equally important skills but sometimes one may be more appropriate than the other or you may need to back up one with the other.

As a very general rule, you need to write things down if what you are trying to record or pass on are facts. Feelings and opinions may be better dealt with face to face. It is usually more complicated than this though, and in this section we'll be looking at some of the considerations one is likely to have to make when deciding whether to write or talk.

2.   Writing Versus Talking

 TIME GUIDE 1 MINUTE

Suppose you need to find out from one of your workteam how he would feel about transferring to another section. You are not in a position to make him a firm offer but you want to sound him out about the idea.

Would you call him over for a chat or send him a note asking for his views in writing?

PART

1

I hope you felt that you would call him over for a chat rather than writing him a note.

The important thing in this situation is to find out his feelings — perhaps what he wanted from his job, perhaps his worries about work. Depending on how the conversation went, you might decide in the end not even to mention the possibility of a transfer to another section.

Or, on the other hand, if you felt strongly that he should accept the transfer to another section, you would probably answer all his arguments and deal with any worries or misunderstandings he might have as they come up.

If you did either of these, you would be very carefully and accurately adjusting the way you put your ideas across and responding to his ideas as the conversation progressed.

This fine adjustment is something which you cannot do if you write to somebody although, of course, you usually have more chance to weigh your words in the first place if you are putting your ideas on paper.

REFERENCE 1
page 91 The differences between spoken and written communication are dealt with in 'The Principles and Practice of Supervisory Management' by David Evans, Chapter 7.

Now let's look at another example.

ACTIVITY 2   TIME GUIDE 3 MINUTES

You receive from the Safety Officer a memo about the importance of wearing goggles to carry out certain cutting operations for which goggles haven't previously been worn.

Would you:

a) Put the Safety Officer's memo on the notice board where your workteam would see it?

b) Tell them in a briefing session about the new requirement to wear goggles while cutting?

c) Tell them individually?

d) Photocopy the Safety Officer's memo and give each of your workteam members a copy?

e) Put up a notice saying 'GOGGLES MUST BE WORN DURING ALL CUTTING OPERATIONS'?

f) Any combination of a, b, c, d or e?

PART

2

There isn't an obvious right answer to this question. Let's look at each possibility in turn:

a) you would certainly have fulfilled your duty to pass on the information from the Safety Officer to your workteam — just about;

b) but research which has been done into how people view information from management suggests that where the subject matter affects them directly (e.g. pay, working conditions, safety) people expect to be *told* by the person for whom they work directly. And in the case of your workteam, that's you. So, in this case, I think you would certainly have to tell them yourself about wearing goggles, and a briefing session, where you can get the whole workteam together, is probably the most effective and economical way to do it;

c) telling them individually would be just as effective but would be very time-consuming for you. However, you might well feel that telling people isn't enough and that you need to reinforce what you say with some written information;

d) in that case we're back to putting the Safety Officer's memo on the board, photocopying individual copies of his memo; or

e) putting up a notice. Notices very quickly become overlooked, particularly something like a memo on a noticeboard which wouldn't be eye-catching in any way. An individual copy put on each team member's desk or directly into his hand might have a better chance of being read. The trouble with this, though, is that there's a tendency to generate far too much paper in all businesses — you may well have suffered from it yourself. And running off however many photocopies your workteam needs in this instance would just be adding to the mountain of unnecessary paper. So a well-written clear notice, clearly displayed by the cutting equipment will probably be the most effective form of written communication in this case;

f) probably what is called for is a combination of spoken and written messages. I would choose telling the workteam in a briefing session and putting up a notice as a reminder of what had been said.

So, we can see from this activity that writing and speaking back each other up, particularly in our dealings with our own workteams.

3. Writing as Back-up

Let's look at another example of using written communication as back-up to a spoken message.

Suppose you have held a briefing session for your group to tell them about the company's proposals to introduce flexible working hours. At the end of the briefing session you give each of them a list of the main points you have made.

Here is an extract from the list.

Proposals for Flexible Working Hours

1. In a four week period you should work 140 hours.

2. Daily hours can be worked between 8 a.m.— 6 p.m.

3. Up to 10 hours credit or debit can be carried forward to the next four week period.

4. Core time (11 a.m.— 3 p.m.) should be worked daily unless you are taking holiday or credit hours carried forward.

5. Hours to be worked daily should ordinarily be arranged one week in advance, in co-operation with your supervisor and workteam.

Jot down some of the benefits for you and your workteam of providing such a list at the briefing session and for them to take away afterwards.

_____

_____

_____

_____

_____

_____

PART

Well, there are all sorts of benefits and it would be hard to put them in a rigid order of priorities.

3.1. Consistent Story

I think I would put first on my list the fact that written information given to several people goes some of the way to ensure that they all go away with the same story.

In the example we've looked at, at least the details of the arrangements for introducing flexible working hours should stay the same in your workteam's discussions because they've got it written down in front of them. If you had just told them about it, the accounting period, number of hours to be worked, core time, etc, would soon be forgotten and re-invented.

If you remember pounds, shillings and pence, you've perhaps heard the story of the verbal message which was passed down the line; it started as:

"Send reinforcements, we're going to advance."

and ended up as:

"Send three and fourpence, we're going to a dance."

It's not only mishearing that distorts a message; each time the story is retold or discussed with a different person, the interpretation of what was said will change a bit.

You can't entirely prevent this by supplying information in writing as well — you can't guarantee that it will be read for a start — but you *will* be doing as much as you can.

3.2. Future Reference

Another benefit of giving everybody a list of information such as we looked at is that, if it's on paper, everybody has the details to refer to later if they want to. A change of working hours involves quite a lot of detailed arrangements: if people have those details on paper in front of them they are more likely to listen to the *ideas* when someone is explaining it to them rather than trying to memorise details — they can always come back to these when they re-read the list.

And they will *need* to re-read the list several times to check up on points when they are thinking about the change in hours. After all, there's a lot to think about. Without a written list they would have nothing to refer to except what they half-remembered hearing.

3.3. A Basis for Discussion

As well as the list containing detailed information which people might like or need to check up on, it also forms the basis for further discussion.

Let's look at two items on that list particularly which might do this.

PART

5

ACTIVITY 4

Write down some of the points which you think you would want more information about or about which you would want to ask questions, if you were given a list of information containing these two items.

4. Core time (11 a.m.–3 p.m.) should be worked daily unless you are taking holiday or credit hours carried forward.

5. Hours to be worked daily should ordinarily be arranged one week in advance, in co-operation with your supervisor and workteam.

_____

_____

_____

_____

_____

If I were given these two items on a list, I should want at least to know:

what was meant by 'core time';

when I could take my lunch break during core time and for how long;

exactly how the supervisor was going to arrange cover in my section.

Without a *written* basis for discussion, talks tend to be rather general and directionless or else you have to explain the same detail several times over before everybody takes it in.

3.4. Treating People Equally

You may have thought that another benefit of giving people information in writing is that they all get the same story *at the same time*. Of course, and in the example we've looked at, if you've held a briefing session and all your workteam attended, the problem of some people knowing before others doesn't arise, but supposing they hadn't all been there? Or supposing senior management had just said to start informing people on a certain day?

PART

6

ACTIVITY 5

Jot down how YOU would feel if you heard about an important issue like a change of working hours a day or two after it was common knowledge to some of your workteam or colleagues in other areas?

_____

_____

_____

_____

_____

_____

You would probably feel pretty fed up and would probably not be prepared to consider the new working hours favourably. This is a very common communication failure in all sorts of businesses and few things irritate people more than finding out information they feel it was their right to hear from their boss from somebody else.

Perhaps it has happened to you at some time and you know how annoying it is.

Putting the information on paper ALONE isn't enough to ensure that everybody feels the situation has been fully explained, but at least if everybody gets their own copy of the information at the same time then management has gone some way to making sure that everybody feels fairly treated.

So, to my mind, the main benefits of written information as back-up in that example are that it gives:

a)   a consistent story;

b)   a record for future reference;

c)   a basis for discussion;

d)   it ensures everybody is treated equally.

And these benefits are generally true when you are giving information to a number of people, whether it's 10 or 1,000.

In the last example we looked at and in the benefits we discussed as arising from providing that written information, we were concentrating mainly on what written communication can do for encouraging good relations between management and the workforce or between you and your workteam.

PART

7

4. Writing for Efficiency

Important though good relations are, we also have to think about what written communications can do for efficiency and three of the benefits we've just discussed come in again here:

a)   a consistent story;

b)   a record for future reference;

c)   a basis for discussion.

ACTIVITY 6 — TIME GUIDE 4 MINUTES

Suppose you call a meeting — perhaps it involves one or two other supervisors, somebody from maintenance and some of your workteam. You don't want the meeting to take longer than about half an hour and you want to make sure that what is decided at the meeting is actually carried out.

What written information would you give the people attending the meeting to make sure that it was as brief and productive as possible?

_____

_____

_____

_____

_____

_____

Well, I would give them two separate documents. One document, given well before the meeting, would tell them what items were to be discussed, in as much detail as they needed to come to the meeting well-prepared.

The second, sent out within twenty-four hours of the meeting if I could possibly manage it, would spell out what had been discussed and agreed and, most importantly, who had agreed to do something about it.

8

These two documents are called the Agenda and the Minutes and they are sometimes very formally written. If you'd like to know more about writing agendas and minutes you may find useful the notes in Part D, Checklists for Business Writing.

It doesn't matter if you never use the terms 'Agenda' and 'Minutes' though. The point is that telling people in advance what's to be discussed in writing, and telling them soon afterwards in writing what's been agreed, gives them:

a)   a basis for discussion;

b)   a record for future reference.

Utilising this approach makes the most effective use of everybody's time, no matter how informal your meeting — provided that you give people enough information to be of use.

Look at this example.

ACTIVITY 7

TIME GUIDE 10 MINUTES

Suppose two people are invited to a meeting and one of the items on the agenda is:

COMMUNICATIONS

One of these people, Jack Bennett, is responsible for the company's telephone switchboard, internal telephones, telex and facsimile transmission, both of which use telephone lines.

The other, Janet Hogarth, works in Publicity and Public Relations and is very keen to start a house magazine.

If they see 'Communications' on the agenda, what are they each likely to think it means and come prepared to discuss?

Jot down your ideas below.

Jack Bennett   _____

                 _____

                 _____

Janet Hogarth   _____

                 _____

                 _____

PART

Well, they'll each come prepared to talk about their own particular interest.

JACK BENNETT is likely to assume the 'Agenda' means COMMUNICATIONS SYSTEM such as telex and facsimile and would expect to talk about them.

JANET HOGARTH would assume 'Communications' meant company communications with its customers, employees or the public. The meeting might give her a chance to get her house magazine off the ground — she would certainly want to talk about it.

But supposing by 'Communications' the Chairman meant that he actually wanted *to discuss current communication problems between departments and to work out some practical solutions*.

Jack Bennett and Janet Hogarth would rightly be annoyed that they had wasted time preparing other information for the meeting and the meeting wouldn't be very productive because they *wouldn't* have prepared their views on what was to be discussed, so it would be a pretty inefficient use of everybody's time.

If the subject italicised above is what the Chairman wanted to discuss at the meeting then that is exactly what he should have put on the agenda.

REFERENCE 2
page 91

This point is dealt with in an effective and entertaining way in the Video Arts film: 'Meetings, Bloody Meetings'.

5.   Passing the Message

Probably if you were going to hold a meeting you would give some thought to what, if anything, you needed to write down beforehand and afterwards.

Many situations in which we ought to write something down, however, take us unawares and, if we're not careful, can cause a lot of damage and expense or an infuriating waste of time for somebody at the very least. Here's an example.

PART

10

ACTIVITY 8

Alan Jenkinson is in the office alone when the telephone rings. It's Dublin Bay Printers Ltd. wanting to speak to Brendan O'Connor about a delivery of printing chemicals which should have arrived three days earlier. They can't afford to wait longer than another twenty-four hours. If delivery can't be guaranteed in that time they'll cancel the order.

Alan Jenkinson goes to lunch at 1.00 p.m. and asks the typist in the next office to keep an eye open for Brendan O'Connor and tell him to ring Dublin Bay Printers. When Brendan O'Connor comes in she tells him a customer was ringing from Dublin or Belfast or somewhere about a missing order.

He doesn't understand the message and anyway, he has a lot or urgent jobs to do.

Next morning a telex arrives cancelling the order.

What ought Alan Jenkinson to have done to ensure that Brendan O'Connor dealt with the problem?

_____

_____

_____

_____

_____

_____

At the very least, he should have taken a proper, written message and put it where Brendan O'Connor was bound to see it. (We don't know that he was in a positiion to do much more, like following the problem up himself or handing it over to somebody more senior.)

So this is one instance where a record can be essential if other people's time is not to be wasted and taking reliable 'phone messages is something that we all need to be reminded about whatever our job.

In general, IF YOU HAVE TO PASS A MESSAGE ON FROM ONE PERSON TO ANOTHER, WRITE IT DOWN.

PART

11

6. Writing to Overcome a Time Lag

Finally, you will need to write information down if there is a time lag between your giving the information and somebody else using it.

ACTIVITY 9
TIME GUIDE 3 MINUTES

Suppose, for example, you are training a new starter in your section. You have time one day to train him in a particular process, but you know you won't require him to do the job for real until perhaps a week later when the pressure on everybody's time might be much greater.

How would you overcome the time lag between the training session and his doing the job?

_____

_____

_____

_____

I would write him a set of instructions to refer to when he actually had to do the job himself. If he had had adequate training to start with, the written instructions should jog his memory sufficiently for him to do the job efficiently. Expecting him to remember what he'd been told a week earlier would be inefficient and unreasonable.

Writing things down takes time which we sometimes feel we can ill-afford, but it _saves_ time in the long run.

Similarly, if you have to give any kind of report on work in your section, whether it's a shift log which you complete and hand on to the next shift or whether it's a one-off special report for your boss, there is going to be a delay between your giving the information and its being used. In the case of a change of shift, it's a matter of hours, in the case of a management development it may be weeks, but the principle is the same.

ACTIVITY 10

TIME GUIDE 3 MINUTES

Suppose that a particular vessel in a production area has been overheating slightly during the nightshift. The nightshift foreman has tested the temperature every hour and although it's only running 10° above normal at the end of his shift, which isn't yet critical, the increase in temperature has risen from 2° above normal to 10° above normal in eight hours.

He could have a word with the foreman on the dayshift — "Keep an eye on Vessel C. It's overheating by about 10°".

OR

He could put a report in the shift log to tell the dayshift when he had tested the vessel, what his findings were and to say that testing should be continued.

What do you think the benefits of a written report would be?

_____

_____

_____

_____

_____

_____

Well, assuming that the dayshift foreman actually reads the log, he should be alerted to the fact that there is a problem developing. If he is just told that the vessel is overheating he's probably going to monitor it for himself for a few hours to see whether the temperature continues to rise and by that time serious damage could be done.

If he has all the recorded temperatures from the nightshift then one more measurement of his own would probably convince him that he should call in maintenance and *they*, thanks to the nightshift foreman's report, would have the whole story which they wouldn't otherwise get.

So these are some of the occasions when you may feel you have a choice as to whether you write or speak, or do both.

PART

I certainly don't recommend generating more paperwork than you have to, but if your aim is to maintain good relations with your workteam and with other people in the company and to work effectively yourself and to get the most effective performance from your workteam, then writing it down can sometimes be just what is needed and will more than pay for the time it takes you to do it.

But how?

We'll be looking at how to write simple, easily understood English in the next section.

First you might like to spend a few minutes checking what we've done so far.

SELF CHECK I

Complete the following statement with a word or group of words.

a) _____ is better for facts and figures, _____ is better for feelings and opinions.

b) If you give a group of people to whom you are speaking some written information they all go away with _____ story.

c) If you give a group of people written information, they will use it for _____ and as _____.

d) Written information given before a meeting makes _____ use of everybody's time.

e) A written summary given to everybody after a meeting helps to make sure that decisions are _____.

f) You should write information down if the message is to be _____ (e.g. a telephone message).

g) You should write information down if there is _____ before somebody uses the information.

RESPONSE CHECKOUT

a) writing is better for facts and figures, speech is better for feelings and opinions;

b) the same — the only way to begin to ensure that what you've said is faithfully discussed afterwards;

c) future reference and points for discussion;

d) efficient or effective;

e) carried out or implemented;

f) passed on to somebody else;

g) a time lag or a delay.

PART

14

7. Summary

● Writing isn't better than speech — they have different functions.

● As a general rule, use writing for facts and figures, and speech for opinions and feelings.

● Use written information to back up what you say if you want:

> a consistent story;
> a record for future reference;
> a basis for discussion;
> to be seen to be fair.

● If you have to pass a message on, WRITE IT DOWN.

● If there will be a time lag between your giving some information and its being used, WRITE IT DOWN.

PART B   HOW TO WRITE

1.   Introduction

Having decided to write then we have to put pen to paper. Most people will tend to put this off as long as possible — a blank sheet of paper can be quite a challenge. It's a common complaint that, although people may feel quite happy talking about any subject under the sun and have no difficulty putting the words together, when they are faced with writing something down — a letter, a report or whatever — the words seem to desert them and they feel clumsy and awkward in the way they string ideas together.

This is partly lack of practice and partly, I think, that when we write, we tend to strive for a more official-sounding, formal style than we use when we talk. This is largely a waste of time — business letters, memos and reports are all the better if they are written as simply and fluently as the writer would normally speak.

Writing simply can be a life's work and it's sometimes tempting to write something careless and *long*. (One famous author began a letter to a friend "I'm writing you a long letter because I haven't time to write a short one".)

However, there are a few key ways in which we can make our writing simple, clear and direct and that's what we'll be looking at in this part of the unit.

Another problem which people find sometimes with writing is that what they write doesn't *sound* like them. It sounds cold, stiff and impersonal — almost as though it was written by a robot rather than a human being.

There are ways of avoiding that too and we'll look at these in the second half of this part of the unit.

2. How to Make Your Writing Simple, Clear and Direct

ACTIVITY II

Suppose you received the following letter:

Dear Sir

With reference to your recent letter, we are now in a position to advise you that your order has been expedited and you should obtain receipt of the outstanding items, namely 21 OHS baffles, by 31st January latest.

Assuring you of our best attention at all times,

Yours faithfully

Jot down what you think about the *way* the letter is written.

_____

_____

_____

What impression do you form of the writer from reading the letter?

_____

_____

_____

(Don't bother about the possible inefficiency which led to the letter being necessary in the first place.)

Well, I think the first thing that strikes one is the pompous language in which the letter is written: "We are now in a position to advise you" and "you should obtain receipt", are just two examples of what I mean — you may well have picked out more.

We UNDERSTAND what the writer is saying but he could have said it far more simply. For example 'you should receive', or 'the order should arrive' would be better than 'you should obtain receipt'. And 'we are now in a position to advise you', could probably have been left out altogether if the sentence had been changed a little.

But worse than this, the writer uses one word, 'expedite', which quite possibly the reader wouldn't understand. In fact, it means 'hurried up', nothing more, but you suspect that the writer is using it to sound important and official.

Trying to make ourselves sound important is an understandable human weakness but it doesn't usually cut much ice! A letter like this is more likely to annoy or amuse the reader rather than impress him.

Finally, the writer uses some old-fashioned flowery phrases which, perhaps, used to be very common in commercial writing, but which have largely been abandoned in the last twenty years or so. I mean 'With reference to' and 'Assuring you of our best attention at all times.'

Beginning something with 'with reference to' tends to involve you in writing a very cumbersome sentence. It's simpler and sounds better to deal with what you are referring to in a separate sentence like this: 'Thank you for you recent letter. I have followed up your order . . .'. And 'Assuring you of our best attention at all times', although it sounds friendly enough, could well be replaced by something simpler like: 'We apologise for the delay', in the example we've been looking at.

So this letter would be much better if the writer:

● **MADE THE POINT AS BRIEFLY AS POSSIBLE;**

● **USED COMMON WORDS RATHER THAN DIFFICULT WORDS;**

● **USED SIMPLE EXPRESSIONS RATHER THAN FLOWERY ONES TO OPEN AND CLOSE THE LETTER**

And if he had done these things the letter might read something like this:

Dear Sir

Thank you for your recent letter.

I have followed up your order for 21 OHS baffles which should reach you before 31st January.

I apologise for the delay.

Yours faithfully

Here's another example of a pompous, wordy piece of writing — this time a memo. Rewrite the memo on the memo form provided making it as simple and to the point as you feel it should be.

MEMORANDUM

FROM: Office Supervisor	TO: All Office Staff
SUBJECT: Training Sessions	DATE: 10 Jan

It has been decided by the Training Officer to hold 1-day training sessions in word processing and the use of the spread-sheet package for all staff wishing to avail themselves of this facility.

I am instructed to ask you to notify me by Friday 18th January of your intention with regard to these courses and to indicate your preferred dates.

The courses will be held on 25th/26th February (Word Processing)
27th/28th February (Spread-sheet)

MCT

MEMORANDUM

FROM: Office Supervisor	TO: All Office Staff
SUBJECT: Training Sessions	DATE: 10 Jan

MCT

PART

19

Everybody is likely to have written something slightly different for this but here is my version for you to compare with yours. You'll see that it's much shorter than the original and has got rid of the more long-winded expressions — but it's quite possible that yours is an improvement on mine.

MEMORANDUM	
FROM: Office Supervisor	TO: All Office Staff
SUBJECT: Training Sessions	DATE: 10 Jan

The Training Officer will be holding 1-day courses on word processing and the use of the spreadsheet package on the following dates:

25th/26th February (Word Processing)
27th/28th February (Spread-sheet)

All staff are invited so, if you would like to attend, would you please let me know which course you are interested in and the date you prefer by Friday 18th January.

MCT

So, I hope we can agree we can improve the standard of what we write straight away if we choose the simplest way of saying what we want. And this always means finding *our own* way of saying something rather than using somebody else's overworked expression.

The problem is that long-winded ways of saying things can become very common and, because we hear and read them so often, it is easy for them to be the first expressions which come to mind when we sit down to write.

REFERENCE 3
page 91

In 'The Complete Plain Words', many more common long-winded expressions are picked up than we have time to look at here.

Here are a few examples of what I mean with a simpler alternative shown beside them.

a large proportion of	— many
at an early date	— soon
at the present moment in time	— currently/now
in consequence	— because

If we try putting these expressions in a sentence we can see that the simpler alternative puts the idea across more effectively and saves time and energy for the writer and the reader.

1. A large proportion of those attending the course had no previous management experience.

    Many of those attending the course had no previous management experience.

2. It was agreed that the group should meet again at an early date.

    It was agreed that the group should meet again soon.

3. We are out of stock at the present moment in time.

    We are currently out of stock.

4. In consequence of the Secretary's resignation, the meeting was postponed for a week.

    Because of the Secretary's resignation, the meeting was postponed for a week.

Incidentally, writing things as simply as possible tends to show up ideas and decisions for what they really are.

Let's look at one of these examples again.

   It was agreed that the group should meet again soon.

That is a statement of what was *really* decided and anybody reading that might reasonably think that the group should have done better and fixed a date for their next meeting. Writing 'at an early date' might just be a not very successful attempt to look more efficient than they really were!

ACTIVITY 13

Here are some more examples of sentences containing long-winded, overworked expressions which can be replaced by simpler, clearer ones. Jot down what you think would be a better word to use in each of these sentences instead of the group of words underlined.

a)   Despite the fact that deliveries of raw materials were late the order was met on time.

_____

b)   This in many cases, proved to be so.

_____

c)   I should like to draw your attention to the fact that I haven't been paid.

_____

d)   We must give due consideration to the staff development programme.

_____

e)   In view of the fact that I am retiring this year, I am of the opinion that somebody else should undertake the long-term project.

_____

f)   All departments, with the exception of Data Processing, were represented.

_____

Here are my suggestions, though other words would do as well in some cases. I've written the whole sentence out each time so that you can see that using a simpler expression improves the sentence and doesn't affect the meaning in any way:

a)   Although deliveries of raw materials were late, the order was met on time.

PART

b)   This <u>often</u> proved to be so.

c)   I should like to <u>point out</u> that I haven't been paid.

d)   We must <u>consider</u> the staff development programme.

e)   <u>Since</u> I am retiring this year, I <u>think</u> that somebody else should undertake the long-term project.

f)   All departments <u>except</u> Data Processing were represented.

If we were writing a checklist for *How to Make your Writing as Long-Winded as Possible* we could say:

Don't think for yourself, use whatever wordy expressions are current (and don't worry too much about the meaning);

if one word will do, use six.

And we could add to that:

Make sure you say the same thing twice wherever possible.

If we look closely at some overworked expressions, we can see that all they are doing is repeating an idea which has already been expressed in a previous word. Here are some examples of what I mean:

the reason why this is so is because;
advance planning;
my own personal opinion.

In any sentence 'the reason is', 'why' and 'because' all convey the same idea — you don't need all three.

And, if we look at 'advance planning', planning *has* to be in advance — you certainly can't plan for what has already happened!

And, looking at 'my own personal opinion', well, whose opinion can mine be except my own? So 'my opinion' should be enough.

PART

ACTIVITY 14 TIME GUIDE 3 MINUTES

Here are some more sentences in which the same idea has been expressed twice. Cross out the word or group of words which you feel is unnecessary.

a) The subject of the Finance Director's address will be about the financial forecast for next year.

b) Every single opportunity will be taken.

c) We will continue to remain staying on course.

d) Every individual person must sign this.

Here are my suggestions:

a) The Finance Director's address will be about the financial forecast for next year; *or* The subject of the Finance Director's address will be the financial forecast for next year.

b) Every opportunity will be taken.

c) We will continue on course; *or*, We will remain on course; *or*, We will stay on course.

d) Every individual must sign this; *or*, Everybody must sign this.

So, it's important to check that, when you write something, you're not just repeating something you've already said in a different way.

Earlier on we said that trying to write simply tends to show up ideas and decisions for what they really are. Conversely, if people want to disguise the truth or if they are simply not very sure of what they are saying, they tend to wrap things up in a blanket of words to put the reader off the track.

Of course, this may not always be deliberate but, as a reader and a writer, it's something against which you must be on your guard.

3. Writing Honestly

Let's look at two kinds of common dishonesty that you sometimes find in writing — this doesn't only apply to the sort of written information we come across at work; political statements are often full of very slippery pieces of writing.

PART

ACTIVITY 15

Read the following statements. They are all about the lack of storage space in a particular section of a factory. But what is the writer trying to suggest about the problem in each statement? Jot down what you feel he is trying to do.

● As is well known, storage space in B Section has been insufficient for a number of months.

_____

_____

● It is evident that present storage arrangements are inadequate.

_____

_____

● It is generally agreed that the problem of the lack of proper storage in B Section must have high priority.

_____

_____

● For obvious reasons, storage problems in B Section must be dealt with speedily.

_____

_____

He's trying to suggest that he has support from other people for the views he is expressing:

"As is well known . . .";

"It is evident that . . ."

"It is generally agreed that . . .".

Now, if he provides *evidence* of that support, we can perhaps accept his argument, but in these particular statements he's not providing any evidence at all, just saying that the support is there. And if a piece of writing containing comments like these arrived on your desk, then you would have to read it very critically.

Similarly, in the last statement, he is suggesting that the reasons for backing up his point of view are so apparent that they don't need saying. That's something which should always be treated with great suspicion.

PART

So one common kind of dishonest writing is

SUGGESTING THAT YOUR ARGUMENT IS BETTER SUPPORTED THAN IT REALLY IS.

The second kind of dishonesty is, I think, even worse and, in my experience, is rarely unintentional.

Let me give you an example of what I mean.

> "In the past year we have made several changes in our personnel structure and streamlined our organisation considerably. These improvements are now beginning to pay off and I'm sure that, in the next quarter, we shall find . . .".

Did you notice that at first the writer refers to "changes" in the personnel structure, but the next time he mentions them in the following sentence he refers to them as "improvements"? And, as we all know, changes aren't necessarily improvements. We would need to be convinced by some evidence that changing the personnel structure had actually brought about some improvements.

ACTIVITY 16   TIME GUIDE 3 MINUTES

Here are two more instances of dishonest writing similar to the example we have just looked at.

Jot down how you think the writer is 'cheating' in each case.

a) 'In the Data Processing department we have the example of a section supervisor who started with the company in Marketing and, following retraining, has moved successfully into Data Processing. I see this trend continuing throughout the company.'

_____

_____

_____

b) 'The manager's opinion is that the fall of the pound against the dollar should increase our sales in the short term. This in fact encourages me to think that . . .'

_____

_____

_____

a)   In the first instance, the writer takes one example (somebody transferring from Marketing to Data Processing) and then describes the example as a trend. I hope we can agree that you need more than one instance to make you believe you have a trend.

b)   In this example, the writer states an opinion in the first sentence and, in the second sentence, he treats this as a fact which, of course, it isn't.

So, our aim should be to write briefly, simply and honestly. But if it's *too* brief and simple, is what we write going to sound boring, even childish? It needn't if we adopt a few simple guidelines which we'll look at now.

4.   How to Sustain Interest and Readability

Most people who have to read anything you write at work will appreciate it if your wording is brief, simple and to the point and are more likely to maintain interest than if the memo or report is wordy and obscure.

As well as choosing simple words and neat phrases, we can also improve the simplicity of our writing by using fairly short sentences. I don't mean by this that they are so short that the writing sounds as though it could have been written by a small child, like this:

The holiday list is now on the board.

Please decide what holidays you want by the end of this month. Check them with your section head to make sure there is no clash of holidays within your section. Section heads will enter them on the list for all staff in their sections.

If you need to make changes later in the year we shall, of course, try to help, but if you want to be sure of having the weeks you want, please fix them early. If you need to make changes once the holiday list is fixed you should see your section head in the first instance.

But, as a general rule, if you are writing something by hand (perhaps to be typed) and you write a sentence which is four lines long or even longer, then the chances are that *you* have lost the thread of what you were saying and so will your reader. But that's a pretty rough guide!

PART

27

4.1. A Reading Index

To give a little more precision to our measurement of how easy to read our writing is we can use a reading index. There are various reading indices which one can use but here is a very simple one.

Take a passage of 100 words.

Here is an example:

> Thank you for your letter of 4 <u>January</u> in which you expressed an <u>interest</u> in the post of first line <u>supervisor</u> in our <u>electronics</u> plant.
>
> We feel that your <u>experience</u> and <u>qualifications</u> may be what we are looking for and we should be very pleased to discuss the post with you.
>
> I suggest we meet here on Friday 1 <u>February</u> at 11 a.m. when my <u>associate</u> Mr Paul, who will be Process <u>Manager</u> of the new plant, will be able to join our <u>discussion</u>.
>
> Please let me know if this date is not <u>convenient</u>, so we can arrange an <u>alternative</u>.

First, you count the number of sentences and work out the average number of words per sentence. You do this by working out the sum

100 divided by the number of sentences

ACTIVITY 17   TIME GUIDE 1 MINUTE

How many sentences are there in this passage? _____

So the average sentence length is $\dfrac{100}{?}$ = _____

There are four sentences in the passage so the average sentence length is $\dfrac{100}{4}$ = 25 words.

Next, you count up the number of words which contain three or more syllables in a group of 100 words. As you can see I have underlined the twelve words of three or more syllables in this passage.

(You notice that I have not included 'expressed' in the first line of the passage which you could argue is a three syllable word. This is because you don't include in your calculations any words which only become three syllables because they end in 'ing', 'ed' or 'es'.)

Finally you add together

the average number of words in a sentence   +   number of words of three or more syllables in a group of 100 words

and this gives you the *readability index*.

So, in the example we're looking at we add:

25 + 12 = 37.

The reading index for this passage is 37 which is about right for a simple business letter. If the reading index for any passage falls between 35–45 you can feel fairly confident that the reading level is suitable for most business purposes.

ACTIVITY 18

TIME GUIDE 10 MINUTES

Work out the reading index for this passage. The words containing three or more syllables have already been underlined.

To counter the <u>hideous</u> <u>spectacle</u> of high and growing <u>unemployment</u> the only <u>solutions</u> offered seem to be "get on your bike", a shorter working week or a shorter working life. Leaving aside the <u>unrealism</u> of the first, the others appear to me (<u>respectively</u>) a <u>formula</u> for <u>overtime</u> payments or a <u>rejection</u> into <u>another</u> kind of <u>unemployment</u> called early <u>retirement</u>. Why, oh why, isn't the power of the training <u>industry</u> marshalled to tackle the problem of the long-term <u>unemployed</u>, that increasing army of those robbed of <u>dignity</u> and hope? Training by its very nature <u>inculcates</u> increased skill and <u>awareness</u> and <u>confidence</u>.

Adapted from 'What strategy?' Dr Frank Metcalfe
Training and Development Volume 3 No 8 December 1984

PART

I make the reading index for that passage 43 — in other words near the top of the scale of what we can reasonably expect to understand without some difficulty.

Of course, you won't have time to apply a readability index to everything you write but it might be quite useful and informative to try it on a few samples of your writing — particularly if you suspect that your style is rather long-winded.

Looking at the reading index confirms that reasonably short sentences and simple words makes our writing easy to understand, but we want it to be a bit more than that. We also want it to be *pleasing* to read.

ACTIVITY 19   TIME GUIDE 3 MINUTES

Look at this passage.

It is brief and simple but the overall effect is of a rather boring piece of writing.

Jot down why you think this is.

> Darlington is a town in North East England. It has a population of 96,000. It is just north of the boundary between Durham and North Yorkshire. Its heyday was in the nineteenth century. It grew with the development of railways in the region. Traditional heavy engineering has now been replaced by light engineering plants and service industries. Unemployment is higher than the national average. It has tended to be less hard-hit by recession than the surrounding areas.

_____

_____

_____

_____

_____

Well, what is 'boring' tends to be a rather personal judgement, but I hope we can agree that this passage isn't very interesting to read because it doesn't flow. The sentences are all of a rather similar length and none of them connects with the sentence which follows, which tends to create a rather jumpy effect.

So, though being careful not to make the sentences too long, we can improve this passage if we run sentences together to make the whole thing flow better.

Darlington is just north of the boundary between Durham and North Yorkshire, in North East England. It has a population of 96,000. It grew with the development of railways in the region and reached its heyday in the nineteenth century. Now traditional heavy engineering has been replaced by light engineering plants and service industries. Although unemployment there is higher than the national average it has tended to be less hard hit by recession than the surrounding area.

I hope you agree that this version reads better than the original.

Notice too that the length of sentences varies more this time. If we count up the words per sentence in this version we find that the passage goes like this:

Number of words per sentence

16
6
18
14
23

and this variety in sentence length and structure makes any written material more interesting to read.

I am not suggesting that you should count up the number of words per sentence when you are writing and make sure that the same number doesn't recur too often! But if you have to write a fairly lengthy piece, a long letter or a report for instance, you *should* be able to make it more interesting reading if you deliberately vary the sentence length and structure somewhat.

REFERENCE 4
page 91

Ways of connecting sentences are dealt with in more detail than we have scope for in "What do you mean 'Communication'?". If you feel you need a refresher on sentence structure you might find it useful to refer to this book.

PART

Here is another example of rather monotonous writing.

Write your own version which flows together better and in which the sentence length is more varied.

Supervisors have always tended to be the 'best' operatives.

This is tradition.

One example is promoting the salesman with the highest turnover to sales supervisor.

Another example is promoting the best toolmaker to toolroom foreman.

Their previous position gives them a special understanding of the problems of the people they now supervise.

Supervisors also need to be able to manage people. Being good at one kind of job doesn't necessarily mean they'll be good at another.

You need training.

_____

_____

_____

_____

_____

_____

_____

_____

PART

It's very unlikely that our improved versions of that passage are the same. But here is mine anyway to compare with yours.

> Traditionally, supervisors have tended to be the 'best' operatives. Thus, the salesman with the highest turnover is promoted to sales supervisor and the best toolmaker is promoted to toolroom foreman. Although their previous position gives them a special understanding of the problems of the people they now supervise, being good at one job doesn't necessarily mean they'll be good at another. For supervisors need to be able to manage people and for that they need training.

I think you'll agree that this (and yours too I hope) is more varied and flows better than the original.

5. Sounding Human

Writing simple, clear letters, memos and reports which read well will do a lot to improve our reputation for communicating well but, as we mentioned at the beginning of this part of the unit, we may still feel that what we write sounds rather cold and impersonal. So how can we get round that problem?

Let's look at a few simple techniques we could use.

5.1. People Matter — Don't Emphasise Things

Look at this pair of sentences:

> Every effort will be made.

> We shall make every effort.

In the first sentence the emphasis is on the *effort* — that is the main idea which we register if we read that sentence. In the second sentence the emphasis is spread between 'we' and 'effort' so we learn from that sentence what is being made ('every effort') and who is doing it ('we').

Sometimes, of course, we *want* to emphasise a thing rather than a person but, as a general rule, if you write in this impersonal way for any length, you create a rather cold, remote effect which doesn't give a very favourable impression.

PART

ACTIVITY 21

Here are two more sentences written in a similar way to the one we've just looked at. Rewrite each sentence so that the emphasis is on the person as much as on the thing. I've given you a start on the first one.

a)   Enquiries will be dealt with by Miss Smith.

Miss Smith will _____

b)   Your application has been received by the Personnel Officer.

_____

_____

I would have completed the first sentence: 'Miss Smith will deal with enquiries' and the second sentence 'The Personnel Officer has received your application'.

Your wording may not be quite the same as mine but I hope it is on the same lines.

Perhaps you can see what I mean about the rather cold, remote effect created by writing which emphasises *things* as opposed to *people* when you read the following.

Dear Sir

Your letter of 10 January has been received and has been passed to the Editorial Section.

Fees are not normally paid but, in this instance, it is felt that consideration should be given to the particular expenses incurred by you as a result of your research. A decision on this, however, will be made by the Editor and will be conveyed to you within a few days.

Your contribution to the journal is appreciated.

Yours faithfully

PART

34

ACTIVITY 22

Rewrite this letter, making sure that the *people* involved are emphasised as much as things like 'fees' and 'decisions' as we did in the previous activity.

Remember also what we have said earlier about writing simply; there's quite a bit of room for improvement in this letter.

_____

_____

_____

_____

_____

_____

_____

_____

_____

My version of the letter looks like this; there will almost certainly be some differences in our choice of wording between yours and mine. However, I hope you find that yours and mine sound more human than the original.

Dear Sir

Thank you for your letter of 10 January which I have passed to the Editorial Section.

We do not normally pay fees but, in this instance, will consider the particular expenses which you have incurred during your research. However, this will be the Editor's decision which I shall let you know within a few days.

Thank you very much for your contribution to the journal.

Yours faithfully

PART

5.2. Don't Hide Behind the Firm

If you look again at my version of the letter in the last activity, you will see that I have used 'I' and 'we', rather than saying 'the Journal', or 'the company', or something similarly anonymous. Thus the second paragraph begins:

'We do not normally pay fees',

and not

'The journal does not normally pay fees'.

This is another way in which we can make what we write sound as though it was written by one human being to another.

I realise that this may not always be easy. Your company may have a house style for letters which makes it difficult for you to use 'I' and 'we' even if you would like to.

And, more than that, you may feel that if you use 'I' you are leaving yourself rather exposed to some personal comeback from what you are writing. But usually the risk isn't that great.

Let's look again for a moment at the last letter we wrote. Here's my version of it again:

> Dear Sir
>
> Thank you for your letter of 10 January which I have passed to the Editorial Section.
>
> We do not normally pay fees but, in this instance, will consider the particular expenses which you have incurred during your research. However, this will be the Editor's decision which I shall let you know within a few days.
>
> Thank you very much for your contribution to the journal.
>
> Yours faithfully

This says that 'I' have passed the letter to the Editorial Section and 'I' will let the correspondent know the Editor's decision within a few days. Neither of those statements is very controversial or likely to get the writer into difficulties.

Everywhere else in the letter I have used 'we', which suggests that it has the backing of the whole organisation but still sounds reasonably friendly. As far as *meaning* is concerned there is very little difference between: 'We do not normally pay fees', and 'It is not normally company policy to pay fees', but there is a considerable difference in the attitude.

PART

36

ACTIVITY 23

TIME GUIDE 3 MINUTES

Here are some more examples of rather cold, impersonal writing.

Improve them by using 'I' and 'we' where you think it is appropriate.

You can also change the wording slightly if you wish — don't forget what we said about emphasising people rather than things.

a) Applications will be dealt with in order of receipt.

_____

b) The decision will be conveyed to you by my secretary.

_____

c) All arrangements will be confirmed by this office.

_____

d) It is regretfully felt that the company are unable to provide further assistance.

_____

_____

Here is how I should rewrite each of these sentences. Of course, your version may differ slightly from mine.

a) We shall deal with applications in the order we receive them.

b) My secretary will let you know the decision.

c) We shall confirm all arrangements.

d) I'm sorry that we're no longer able to help; *or*, I'm sorry that we can't help any further.

PART

5.3. Technical Reports — an Exception

There is one possible exception to what we've said about it being preferable to write emphasising the person rather than concentrating entirely on what's being done. That is if you are writing a technical report.

For a long time, it has been common to write reports in a form which didn't actually mention yourself. Thus you would say:

'Clocking-on procedure was observed fourteen times.'

rather than

'I observed clocking-on procedure fourteen times.'

Once you get used to writing in this impersonal way, it's still possible to write something clear, interesting and lively which doesn't sound as though it was produced by a robot, but it's something which many people find difficult.

If you are writing a fairly straightforward report (perhaps in the form of a memo) to your immediate boss, I think I would still use 'I' rather than writing in an impersonal form. Unless, of course, there is a rule in your company about writing reports in this way.

I think:

> 'I discussed the proposals fully with the entire workteam in B section and we reached the following conclusions . . .';

sounds just as clear and efficient and more human than:

> 'The proposals were fully discussed with the workteam in B section and the following conclusions were reached . . .'.

And most people find it easier to write referring directly to themselves too.

5.4. The Personal Touch

Finally, we can often make what we write sound more human if we spend a few moments adding a personal touch — even to an everyday memo.

I *don't* mean by this that we should write in a gossipy style like this:

> 'I observed clocking-on on the nightshift fourteen times. Jolly cold it was too! Still, here are the results anyway.'

TIME GUIDE 2 MINUTES

But look at these two memos.

Both convey the same information, but which would you prefer to have? Which do you think would create a more favourable impression with the people receiving it?

MEMORANDUM

From A Briggs Quality Circle Leader	To Quality Circle Members
Subject Machine downtime project meeting	Date 1 Jun

The next meeting to discuss the machine downtime project will be this Thursday 2.00 pm in the Committee Room. Please let me know if you are unable to attend.

AB

MEMORANDUM

From A Briggs Quality Circle Leader	To Quality Circle Members
Subject Machine downtime project meeting	Date 1 Jun

Thank you for the encouraging response to this project which I've received since the last meeting.

The next meeting will be on Thursday 2.00 pm in the Committee Room when I hope we can discuss your findings more fully.

Please let me know if you are unable to attend and I'll make sure you are kept informed of developments.

AB

PART

I think the second memo sounds friendlier and more encouraging, yet the effort to write a memo like that rather than the first one takes only a minute or two.

Sometimes the addition of a single sentence is enough to achieve the same effect:

'Thank you for your letter of . . .'.

'Thank you for your support'.

'I look forward to seeing you at the next meeting on . . .'.

'Please let me know if I can be . . .'.

'If you need any further help please . . .'.

Any of these may be suitable to assure whoever you are writing to that *you* are human and that you realise *they* are too.

And, once you get into the habit of including a comment like these, it becomes an almost automatic response and not something over which you have to chew your pen for hours!

ACTIVITY 25   TIME GUIDE 5 MINUTES

Here are the texts of two memos.

I've left plenty of space around the text for you to add a few words or a sentence which you feel would make them both sound more personal and more likely to get a favourable response from the readers.

MEMORANDUM	

From B Johnson
        Supervisor
	To S Woolley
	     QC Manager

Subject
        Staff Turnover
	Date
	     7 May

Here is the analysis of staff turnover May 1980—December 1984 in my section.

I am still waiting for data from personnel for the remaining period.

BJ

PART

40

MEMORANDUM	
From John Evans Training Officer	To Supervisors
Subject Training Plans	Date 2 Nov

Following our meeting I have drawn up training proposals for your sections. Copies, which have also been sent to section superintendents, are attached.

JE

Here is how I would change these two memos to give them a more personal touch.

MEMORANDUM	
From B Johnson Supervisor	To S Woolley QC Manager
Subject Staff Turnover	Date 7 May

Here is the analysis of staff turnover May 1980–December 1984 in my section.

I am still waiting for data from personnel for the remaining period and will let you have the figures as soon as they are available.

BJ

PART

<table>
<tr><td colspan="2" align="center">MEMORANDUM</td></tr>
<tr><td>From John Evans
     Training Officer</td><td>To
    Supervisors</td></tr>
<tr><td>Subject
    Training Plans</td><td>Date
    2 Nov</td></tr>
</table>

MEMORANDUM	
From John Evans Training Officer	To Supervisors
Subject Training Plans	Date 2 Nov

Thank you for your contribution to the meeting last week. I have now drawn up training proposals for your sections and shall be glad to discuss them with you. Copies, which have also been sent to section superintendents, are attached.

JE

What you do to *make* these memos seem more personal is obviously a matter of individual judgement, but I hope we can agree that much that we write in business is improved by making it clear that there was a human being behind it.

You might find it useful to answer the following self check questions now before we go on to look at getting our ideas organised when we write.

SELF CHECK 2   TIME GUIDE 10 MINUTES

1. Here is a list of expressions which can be put more simply. Write a simpler word or group of words beside each one.

   a) in advance of meeting with   _____

   b) in spite of the fact that   _____

   c) ahead of schedule   _____

   d) took into consideration   _____

   e) in view of the fact that   _____

2. Rewrite the following sentence so it is simpler and more friendly.

   With reference to your letter of 25 February, I regret to point out that applications for the post closed on 20 February.

PART

42

3. In each of the three following statements one idea has been expressed twice. Cross out whatever words you think are unnecessary.

    a) Manning levels will continue to remain the same.

    b) I may possibly go home soon.

    c) He tentatively suggested the following changes.

4. Read the following statements. Why is the writer 'cheating'?

    a) It is a well-known fact that men tire more quickly than women in routine manufacturing operations. Therefore we should employ . . .

    b) It is generally agreed that overtime working is unavoidable and since this is so . . .

    c) Several changes have been made in the layout of the Production Department. These improvements have enabled us to establish a small packing area . . .

5. Rewrite the following statements so that the writer is not 'hiding behind' the company.

    The company does not normally deal directly with the public and it is usually recommended that you contact the retailer first. However, since the problem is urgent, a replacement unit will be sent to you directly from this office.

RESPONSE CHECKOUT

The expressions in the first question could all be written more simply like this:

a) before meeting;

b) despite;

c) early;

d) considered;

e) since.

What we would say in response to question 2 will obviously vary but my version would be something like this: Thank you for your letter of 25 February. I regret that applications for the post closed on 20 February.

In question 3:

a) you could either cross out 'continue' or 'to remain';

b) cross out 'possibly' — if you *may* go home soon it's only a possibility anyway;

c) cross out 'tentatively' — a suggestion is tentative in any case.

4.

a) He suggests that his argument is well-supported, ('It is a well-known fact'), but doesn't give any evidence for this;

b) Same criticism as a). There's no evidence given that overtime working is unavoidable;

c) He refers to 'changes' as 'improvements' without showing us why they were improvements.

5. Your wording may differ slightly from mine:

'We do not normally deal directly with the public but suggest you contact the retailer first. However since the problem is urgent, we will send you a replacement unit directly.'

6.   Summary

You can make your writing simple, clear and direct by:

● avoiding lengthy, overworked words and phrases;

● using your own words rather than what is currently fashionable;

● avoiding saying the same thing twice;

● writing honestly.

To write honestly you should:

● not suggest your argument is better supported than it is;

● not change

  opinions into facts,

  changes into improvements,

  example into trend,

  without providing evidence.

To maintain the reader's interest in your writing you should:

● write fairly short sentences;

● write sentences of varying length and structure.

To measure how easy to understand your writing is you can apply a reading index to a passage of 100 words. Simple business writing should have a reading index of between 35 and 45.

● A simple reading index is the average number of words in a sentence + number of words of 3 or more syllables.

To make your writing sound human:

● emphasise the people in your sentences rather than the things, i.e. write actively rather than passively;

● use 'I' and 'we' rather than writing impersonally (with the possible exception of technical reports);

● try to include a personal touch, a recognition of the reader's involvement in memos and letters.

PART

45

PART C
GETTING YOUR IDEAS
ORGANISED

1. Introduction

So far we've looked at why we write and the circumstances in which we might need to write. Also how we can write in a simple, correct and friendly way so that the reader understands what we are saying and, we hope, responds favourably.

But simple, straightforward writing alone isn't enough if our thinking is muddled. So, finally, we must look at how we can organise our ideas and then lay out what we're writing in a way which makes it easy for the reader to see the plan behind it.

2. Why Am I Doing This?

EXTENSION 1
page 90
To start to organise our thinking, when we know we have to write something (perhaps a letter, report or memo) the first thing we must do is ask ourselves *why* we are writing it? What is the purpose of what we are about to write?

This need only take seconds — it doesn't mean that you have gloomily to review the whole of your working life!

PART

46

ACTIVITY 26

Look at these written messages.

Jot down what you think is the purpose of each one.

a)

TELEPHONE MESSAGE
Time Received: 11.20   Date: 11/12 From: H Williams — Hay Engineering 67694
The ARAC14 bearings were despatched by road this a.m. Should arrive before noon tomorrow.
Received by: R.E.

_____

_____

_____

b)

MEMORANDUM	

From:
    Office Supervisor
	To:
	    All Office Staff

Subject:
    Holiday Timetable
	Date:
	    1st Feb

I should like to complete the holiday timetable for this year by the end of the week.

Would you please complete the attached form and return it to me by Friday. Please see me if there are any problems.

Thanks.

                                         R.H.

PART

c)

```
+------------------------------------------------------------+
|                       SAFETY GUIDE                         |
|                                                            |
|                                                            |
|  3.  ... must be thoroughly understood by each employee.   |
|                                                            |
|  4.  NOTIFICATION                                          |
|                                                            |
|      The supervisor in charge of an area where an emergency|
|      occurs is responsible for ensuring that his immediate |
|      superior is notified as soon as possible. The         |
|      superintendent will ensure that the Departmental      |
|      Manager, Safety Engineer and Plant Engineer are       |
|      notified.                                             |
|                                                            |
|  5.  SECURITY GUARD FUNCTIONS                              |
|                                                            |
|      Because the guard must remain at the factory          |
|      entrance ...                                          |
+------------------------------------------------------------+
```

d)

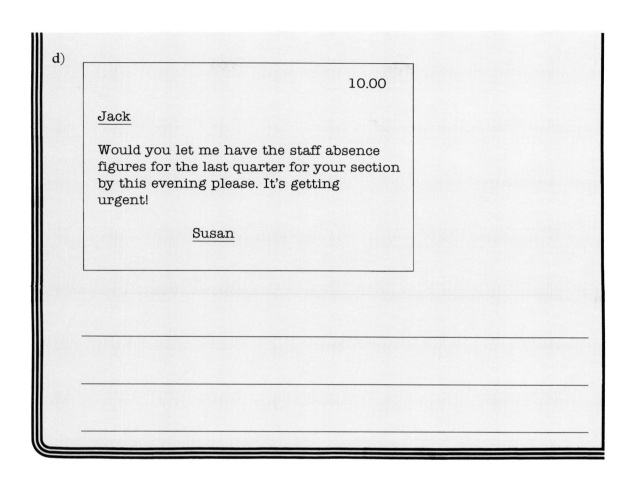

You may have noticed other points but I think the *purpose* of them is that a) and c) are giving information and b) and d) are asking for information.

I think you'll find that anything we write comes in one or both of these categories — we are giving information or asking the reader to give us information or to make some other kind of response.

2.1. Giving Information

So, if we're giving information we next have to ask ourselves: "How much does the reader need to know?"

ACTIVITY 27

Here is a selection of telephone messages.

Below each one jot down what additional information the person receiving the message would need to know.

a)

```
                    11.15 Mon.

    John

    Your wife rang.

                    Roger
```

_____

_____

b)

```
    John

    Will you ring Mr A Hamlin
    77300, Ext 22 as soon as
    possible.

                    RM
```

_____

_____

c)

```
                    Mon 10.05

    John

    The Somerset County
    contract is off. Cancel any
    further runs.
```

_____

_____

d)

```
                    Mon 3.20
    John

    Barton Electronics rang.
    There's a query on the
    order for rev. counters.
    Will you ring them
    (0325 776974) as soon as
    possible.
                    JM
```

_____

_____

PART

a) He'd need to know why his wife rang and whether he should ring her back.

b) He'd need to know when the message was received and what he is supposed to ring back about. It's possible also that a name and number may not mean a lot to John — he should be told the name of the company too.

c) He'd need to know who this message was from and who had received the message.

d) He'd need to know who to telephone at Barton Electronics.

So we can see that none of those telephone messages is altogether efficient and a few moments thought by the person taking the telephone call could save quite a bit of wasted time.

Taking telephone messages is one of the most elementary kinds of writing that we have to do at work. Often, we'd expect to have to give rather more thought to deciding how much the reader needed to know, though the principle remains the same.

ACTIVITY 28   TIME GUIDE 5 MINUTES

Suppose you have to write a report on the success, or lack of it, of introducing flexible working hours into your section. You will have to mention:

● any increase or loss of productivity;

● any difficulties you have found in running the flexible hours system;

● your analysis of the attitudes of your workteam to the new system.

You have all the information you need to hand but what do you need to know before you start to write? Jot down two points on which you would have to be clear before you started writing.

_____

_____

_____

_____

_____

_____

PART

Our answers to this may vary but I suggest that you would need to know:

Who was going to read your report (presumably you would give it to your immediate boss, but the kind of information you would include would depend on who *else* was going to read it or what use was going to be made of it).

How much your readers already know about the subject. For instance, are they likely to be familiar with the precise flexible hours system you've been operating or do you need to describe it in some detail?

So, if we're giving information we need to know who it's for and how much the reader already knows about the subject. Even if we feel confident that the reader will be fairly familiar with what we're going to say, it still helps if you jog his memory with an introductory reading, or a brief introductory sentence or (if it's a report) a short paragraph which sums up the work done to date.

Here are some examples of what I mean:

Dear Sir

Interactive Video Training

I was interested to read of the development of...

MEMORANDUM

From: Production Manager	To: All Supervisors
Subject: Mechanised Production Scheduling	Date: 1st Jun

Further to our meeting with G Thomas last week at which we agreed to use the computer for production scheduling from 1st July, he has arranged a series of training sessions for all production personnel...

PART

2.2. Asking For a Response

And if the purpose of our writing is to get a response from the readers, then we need to make it as straightforward as possible for them to do what we want.

For example, suppose you have a workteam of thirty people and you are trying to arrange the holiday timetable so that you have enough staff to cover at all times.

Thirty people's holiday requirements is too complicated to scribble down on the back of an envelope! And you would be left with quite a time-consuming analysis of dates if you just asked them all to write down the dates they required.

Moreover, they will be more likely to respond if you give them each a form showing all the dates available and asking them just to tick the weeks they would like.

2.3. Encouraging a Response

Sometimes it isn't really practicable to provide for people to respond in this way but you can often at least *encourage* the response you want in a few words.

Here's an example of what I mean:

Suppose, to complete your records you need some figures from various departments in your company. You send out a memo to the departments involved. You are *more* likely to get the response you want if your memo ends —

> "Please let me know if there will be any difficulty providing the figures by Friday"

— than if you simply ask for the information by Friday, because you have given an *encouragement* to the reader to respond.

I realise that, in practice in a case like this, you would probably *still* find yourself telephoning slow departments or having to go round them in person on Friday afternoon!

PART

53

Here are three different situations in which you have to ask somebody to do something. In each one you want to encourage a particular response.

On the blank memo form for each one, write the text of the memo. (You'll see that the details at the top have already been filled in.) Each memo needs only to be two or three sentences long.

a) You want to know numbers being sent to a training session on new products. You are aiming to get three people from each supervisor's section. The sessions will be held on 2nd November — details have already been circulated. The cost of training is charged out to user departments.

b) You are safety representative for your plant and you are letting supervisors know when you want to make a regular safety inspection in their area. As you haven't had the job long you really want the supervisors to join you on the inspection and point out any possible hazards or problems they have come across.

c) You are secretary of your company's Welfare Association. Attendance at committee meetings is often poor and you want to get a better turn-out at the next meeting in the canteen on 9th November at 7.00 p.m. You want to be sure that every department is represented and wonder whether, if the usual representatives can't come, they could arrange for somebody else to.

a)

MEMORANDUM	

From:
    Training Officer
	To:
	    All Supervisors

Subject:
    Product knowledge
    training
	Date:
	    8 May

b)

MEMORANDUM	

From:
  Safety Representative
	To:
	  All Supervisors

Subject:
  Safety Inspection
	Date:
	  11 Feb

c)

MEMORANDUM	

From:
  Secretary — Welfare
  Association
	To:
	  All Supervisors

Subject:
  W A Committee
  Meeting
	Date:
	  1 Apr

Here is what I would write for each of those memos. Quite possibly we have used different ways of encouraging the response we wanted. That doesn't matter. I hope we can agree though that giving a few moments' thought to *how* you can encourage a response is more likely to result in an *effective* piece of communication.

a)

MEMORANDUM	

From:
    Training Officer
	To:
	    All Supervisors

Subject:
    Product knowledge
    training
	Date:
	    8 May

I need to finalise numbers for the training sessions on new products on 2nd November, details of which I sent you last week.

I should be grateful if you would let me know definite numbers by Friday. If I don't hear from you I'll assume you are sending three people from each section and will charge out accordingly.

                BP

b)

MEMORANDUM	

From:
    Safety Representative
	To:
	    All Supervisors

Subject:
    Safety Inspection
	Date:
	    11 Feb

I should like to make a routine safety inspection in each area of the plant next Monday morning, 16th February.

I should be very grateful if you would spare the time to join me on the inspection and should welcome any suggestions or problems which you are able to point out.

                AB

PART

56

```
┌─────────────────────────────────────────────────────────────────┐
│                        MEMORANDUM                                 │
├─────────────────────────────────────────────────────────────────┤
│ From:                              To:                            │
│     Secretary — Welfare                All Supervisors            │
│     Association                                                   │
├─────────────────────────────────────────────────────────────────┤
│ Subject:                           Date:                          │
│     W A Committee                      1 Apr                      │
│     Meeting                                                       │
├─────────────────────────────────────────────────────────────────┤
│ The next meeting of the Welfare Association Committee will be     │
│ held on Thursday 9th November at 7.00 pm in the canteen.          │
│                                                                   │
│ I do hope you will be able to attend. If you are not able to do   │
│ so this time, perhaps you would ask somebody from your            │
│ department to come instead of you.                                │
│                                                                   │
│ It would be very helpful if you would let me know by Friday who   │
│ will be coming from your department.                              │
│                                                                   │
│                                                            KB     │
└─────────────────────────────────────────────────────────────────┘
```

3.   Structure

So, having decided what is the basic purpose of whatever we're writing, and thought in terms of who we are giving information to and why or what we want them to do, we are finally left with the problem of how to put the writing together — the structure.

This isn't a problem if we are writing something very brief but it can take a bit more thinking about if we have to handle several items of information. And usually, that thinking process, getting our own ideas in order, will take care of the structure.

Here's an example of what I mean.

Imagine that we run a large hotel with conference facilities. Here is a list, arranged alphabetically, of the services which we can provide in the conference rooms.

PART

Back projection system — available at an additional charge

Blackboard and easel — provided inclusive of room hire

Flip chart, pads and pens — provided inclusive of room hire

Free-standing lectern — " " " " "

Fruit squash — " " " " "

Iced water — " " " " "

Mineral water — " " " " "

Mints — " " " " "

35mm slide projector — available at an additional price

16mm sound projector — " " " " "

Overhead projector — provided inclusive of room hire

Pads and pencils — provided inclusive of room hire

P A System — available at an additional price

Photocopying — available at an additional price

Secretarial service — " " " " "

Telex — " " " " "

Looking at this list would certainly tell you what facilities are available but could it be organised more helpfully — could it be better structured?

PART

58

ACTIVITY 30

Jot down how you would reorganise the list so that it was more use to a client reading it.
(There's no need to write out all the items on the list.)

_____

_____

_____

_____

_____

_____

_____

I hope we can agree that, although the list *is* organised in one way, in that it is alphabetically arranged, it isn't very useful as it stands.

I would reorganise it like this, separating items which are included in the room hire from those for which an additional charge is made. Notice also that I would group drinks and mints under one heading — refreshments.

Facilities provided inclusive of room hire

Blackboard and easel
Flip chart, pad and pens
Free-standing lectern
Overhead projector
Pads and pencils
Refreshments — fruit squash, iced water, mineral water, mints

Facilities provided at an additional price

Back projection system
35 mm slide projector
16mm sound projector
P A system
Photocopying
Secretarial service
Telex

PART

C

And this is basically how we structure any amount of information which we have to write down for somebody else.

GROUP ITEMS WHICH BELONG TOGETHER:

PUT THEM TOGETHER UNDER A HEADING WHICH MAKES CLEAR WHAT THAT SECTION IS ABOUT.

What isn't clear from the last activity, though, is one other important stage in our organisation.

ACTIVITY 31   TIME GUIDE 3 MINUTES

Suppose we are writing a letter to a client explaining what the hotel's conference facilities are, the costs and the dates on which they are available. We have already grouped the items under these headings.

<u>24 hour conference package</u>

* Special deal available from January 1st. 24 hour conference package includes full use of conference facilities and accommodation in single rooms with private bathroom, breakfast, coffee, lunch, tea, dinner at £8 per head — strongly recommended.

<u>Costs</u>

* Conference suite is hired per part day (maximum 5 hours)
                  or per day   (maximum 12 hours)
* Whole, one third or two thirds of conference suite may be hired— price list available
* Seminar rooms hired separately — £15 per part day each
                               £20 per whole day each
Coffee, tea, buffet, lunch, dinner available. Five possible menus — menus with price per head available.

<u>Dates available</u>

* 20th October, 27th October
* 14th November
* Any date after 12th January

<u>Conference facilities</u>

* Conference suite — conference room 54' 6" × 17' 6" with own
* cloakroom and toilet
* Can be divided into 2 or 3 smaller rooms
* 12 small seminar rooms each seating 12 people
* Some equipment included in room hire — list available
* Additional services charged separately — list available

What decision would you have to make about the groups of information before you could write the letter?

PART

60

You would have to decide *which order* to put them in.

In almost all business writing you start with the most important item and work down to the least important. Most people who are at work feel they have more than enough paperwork to read and, if you didn't make the important points early, they might never read far enough to find them.

Sometimes there isn't one group of information which is clearly more important than another. (You may think that is the case in the example we're looking at. Costs, available dates or the facilities available could *each* be the most important factor to the reader — it depends what the particular circumstances are.)

Usually, however, there is one group of information which has to come first, if what is to follow is to make sense to the reader. That is probably the case in the example we're looking at.

ACTIVITY 32   TIME GUIDE 3 MINUTES

Jot down the order in which you would deal with the groups of information in your letter to the client.

(You need only write down the heading for each group.)

_____

_____

_____

_____

_____

This is the order in which I would deal with the information in the letter:

> Conference facilities;
> Costs;
> 24 hour conference package;
> Dates available.

When you make a choice like this, obviously some personal judgement enters into it, but I hope we can agree that the letter wouldn't make much sense unless we first explained what conference facilities we could offer.

If you glance back at the groups of information about the hotel's conference facilities you will notice that, within each group, the items of information are already in a logical order and it should be fairly straightforward to use them as the basis for a letter.

PART

Often, of course, individual items of information will still be jumbled up even after we have sorted them into groups.

Here is an example.

Conference facilities

    * Conference suite has its own cloakroom and toilets

    * Conference suite is called the Penshaw Suite

    * It can be divided into 2 or 3 smaller rooms

    * The conference room measures 54′ 6″ × 17′ 6″ × 10′

    * The conference room can seat 120

A * There are 12 syndicate rooms

    * If the conference suite is divided the dimensions are:
       two thirds room 36′ × 17′6 × 10′
       one third room 18′ × 17′6 × 10′

A * Each syndicate room seats 12

    * The conference room can accommodate 100 for a buffet or 80 for lunch or dinner

A * Each syndicate room has its own bathroom

But the principle for organising the information is the same.

We group items which belong together and then arrange them in order of importance. And to save writing a lot of information out again we can often do this by simply putting a letter of the alphabet beside items which belong together.

I've already put 'A' beside points referring to syndicate rooms.

ACTIVITY 33

TIME GUIDE 2 MINUTES

Put a letter against the items on the list of conference facilities which you think belong together.

PART

In this example I would say that these topics are covered:

the conference suite;

the dimensions;

the seating capacity;

the syndicate rooms.

Conference facilities

B2 * Conference suite has its own cloakroom and toilets

B1 * Conference suite is called the Penshaw Suite

B3 * It can be divided into 2 or 3 smaller rooms

C1 * The conference room measures 54′ 6″ × 17′ 6″ × 10′

D1 * The conference room can seat 120

A1 * There are 12 syndicate rooms

C2 * If the conference suite is divided the dimensions are:
        two thirds room 36′ × 17′6 × 10′
        one third room 18′ × 17′6 × 10′

A2 * Each syndicate room seats 12

D2 * The conference room can accommodate 100 for a buffet or 80 for
        lunch or dinner

A3 * Each syndicate room has its own bathroom

My list of the conference facilities would be as above. Check your letters with mine but don't worry if they do not entirely match — we may just have taken a different view of the information.

You can see if you look at my list that within each letter group, A, B, C, D I have now added a number to each item. That shows the order in which I would make each of those points as I was writing the letter.

So, if we take group B which contains the following points:

B2 ★ Conference suite has its own cloakroom and toilet;

B1 ★ Conference suite is called the Penshaw Suite;

B3 ★ It can be divided into 2 or 3 smaller rooms.

PART

I should write them up something like this:

> Our conference room, which is called the Penshaw Suite, has its own cloakroom and toilets and can be divided into two or three smaller rooms if required.

ACTIVITY 34

TIME GUIDE 1 MINUTE

Look again at your list of points about the hotel's conference facilities and jot down the order in which you would deal with each letter.

My list would start with 'B'.

My list would be like this: B; C; D; A; though it is possible to do it other ways.

Having decided that I should write that information up something like this.

Our conference room, the Penshaw Suite, has its own cloakroom and toilets and can be divided into two or three smaller rooms as required.

The whole room measures 54′ 6″ × 17′ 6″ × 10′.

But when divided, the two thirds room provides accommodation 36′ × 17′6″ × 10′ and the one third room provides accommodation measuring 18′ × 17′6″ × 10′.

The Penshaw Suite seats 120 people for meetings or a maximum of 100 for buffet service or 80 for lunch or dinner.

We also have 12 syndicate rooms, each seating 12 people and each with its own bathroom.

PART

ACTIVITY 35

Here is a list of points about the *24 hour conference package*

---

24 hours conference package

* full use of conference facilities
* strongly recommended
* accommodation in single rooms with private bathrooms
* coffee and tea are provided during conference
* price includes full English breakfast, lunch and dinner
* available from January 1st
* price is £44 per head
* single rooms have colour television, radio, telephone, tea and coffee making facilities and mini bar
* represents extremely good value for money

---

1. Letter the points which belong together.

2. Decide the order in which you would write up the points in each group and number them.

3. Jot down the order in which you would write up the lettered groups.

I should organise the information about the 24 hour conference package like this though your version may well differ from mine.

---

24 hours conference package

B1	*	full use of conference facilities
A1	*	strongly recommended
C2	*	accommodation in single rooms with private bathrooms
B2	*	coffee and tea are provided during conference
C1	*	price includes full English breakfast, lunch and dinner
A2	*	available from January 1st
D1	*	price is £44 per head
C3	*	single rooms have colour television, radio, telephone, tea and coffee making facilities and mini bar
D2	*	represents extremely good value for money

PART

And I should write up the lettered groups in the following order.

A

B

C

D

This section of my letter would probably look something like this:

May I strongly recommend our special 24-hour conference package which is available from January 1st.

> This would enable you to have full use of the conference facilities including tea and coffee whilst the conference is taking place, and it also includes full English breakfast, lunch and dinner and overnight accommodation in single rooms. Each single room has a private bathroom, colour television, radio, telephone, tea and coffee making facilities and a mini-bar.

> I'm sure you will agree that, at £44 a head, this represents excellent value for money.

A structure plan like we have just been using can help us a little further too.

Let's go back for a minute and have another look at part of a letter I wrote from the plan a few pages back.

Here is the extract again.

Our conference room, the Penshaw Suite, has its own cloakroom and toilets and can be divided into two or three smaller rooms as required.

The whole room measures 54' 6" × 17' 6" × 10'.

But when divided, the two thirds room provides accommodation 36' × 17'6" × 10' and the one third room provides accommodation measuring 18' × 17'6" × 10'.

The Penshaw Suite seats 120 people for meetings or a maximum of 100 for buffet service or 80 for lunch or dinner.

We also have 12 syndicate rooms, each seating 12 people and each with its own bathroom.

Although this contains all the information about the conference facilities in a logical order the layout could be improved so that the reader can see at a glance any particular information he is looking for.

ACTIVITY 36

Jot down two ways in which you think the layout of this part of the letter could be improved.

_____

_____

_____

_____

I would improve it in the following ways — you may have thought of other possibilities as well:

use headings and sub-headings for each new topic;

number the paragraph and the sub-sections in the paragraph;

put the information containing figures together and arrange the figures in vertical columns.

So I feel a better laid out version of the extract would look like this.

1.   Conference facilities

1.1   The Penshaw Suite

Our conference room, the Penshaw Suite, has its own cloakrooms and toilets and can be divided into two or three smaller rooms if required.

1.2   Dimension

Whole room	54'6" × 17'6" × 10'
Two thirds room	36' × 17'6" × 10'
One third room	18' × 17'6" × 10'

1.3   Seating Capacity

The Penshaw Suite seats 120 people for meetings or a maximum of 100 for buffet service of 80 for lunch or dinner.

1.4   Syndicate Rooms

We also have 12 syndicate rooms, each seating 12 people and each with its own bathroom.

PART

C

Let's look at each of these points separately for a moment.

Using headings and sub-headings

If you use a structure plan such as we've already looked at, what the headings and sub-headings could usefully be called is usually fairly obvious.

Using them makes your plan easy for the reader to identify and helps to transfer the information readily to his mind.

You certainly should use headings and sub-headings in reports and memos, and it's becoming quite usual to do so if you are writing a letter which contains quite a bit of detailed information.

Numbering paragraphs and sub-sections of paragraphs

In the same way as headings and sub-headings provide a framework for the reader, so do numbered paragraphs and sub-sections help the reader to pick out which points belong together.

It also makes it easy to refer to particular parts of the document if you are discussing it later. It's quicker and easier to say 'In section 3.5 you mention that . . .' rather than saying 'When you discuss mechanisation you mention that . . .' 'Mechanisation' could appear anywhere in the document and time is lost while everybody leafs through the report or whatever to find the right item.

You notice that I've used a decimal numbering system which is simpler and more consistent than something like 1a, 1b, 2a, 2b, etc., where it's possible, in a fairly lengthy document to become confused about which letter belongs with which number.

Using a decimal system each number (1.3, 23.4 or whatever) will only appear once, and will relate to only one sub-section.

One point to remember with a decimal system is that it's only the figures *after* the decimal point which change in any one section. So after 1.9, you continue 1.10, 1.11, 1.12 — and don't start to number 1.9, 2.0, 2.1.

Arrange figures in vertical columns

Because of the way we have been taught to handle figures, we find it easier to compare two or more figures or to relate them to each other if they are shown to us vertically rather than presented in amongst a line of words.

So, if you are writing something which involves several figures try to arrange them in a simple vertical table.

ACTIVITY 37

TIME GUIDE 10 MINUTES

On the blank memo form provided rewrite the following memo, improving the layout so that the reader can take in the information more easily.

MEMORANDUM

From: R Woolley, Unit Manager	To: All Section Leaders
Subject: Telephone Costs	Date: 3 Sep

I am very concerned about all our rapidly increasing telephone costs. The bill for this quarter is over £1800 compared with £1200 this time last year — an increase of over 50%.

Bills for the other two quarters this year were approximately £1400 and £1500 confirming the upward trend.

We expected that our telephone sales drive would increase costs by 10% and there has, of course, also been a 12% increase in charges this year. Nevertheless we must do something to reduce the remaining 28% increase from this quarter.

Would you please encourage all staff in your section to avoid making calls during the peak rate period 9 a.m.–1 p.m. as much as possible. You might also stress the benefits of preparing for a call before making it so that time spent on the telephone is kept to a minimum. It would also help if staff got into the habit of ringing back or leaving a message rather than holding the line if the person they are calling is not immediately available.

We have never previously attempted to prevent staff making or receiving personal calls — in a small plant like ours there has to be some give and take. I should be grateful, though, if you would ask staff to keep personal calls to a minimum and to use the pay phone in the canteen as far as possible.

RW

PART

MEMORANDUM	
From:	To:
Subject:	Date:

I would lay the memo out like this but, of course, you may have decided to do it slightly differently.

MEMORANDUM	
From: 　　R Woolley, Unit Manager	To: 　　All Section Leaders
Subject: 　　Telephone Costs	Date: 　　3 Sep 85

1. I am very concerned about our rapidly increasing telephone costs — over 50% in the past year as you can see from the figures below.

    Sep '85　　£1800
    May '85　　£1550
    Jan '85　　£1400
    Sep '84　　£1200

2. <u>Reasons</u>

    We forecast an increase of 10% as a result of our telephone sales drive and there has been a 12% increase in telephone charges this year.

3. <u>Reduction of costs</u>

    In order to do something about the remaining 28% increase from this quarter would you please encourage all staff in your section to:

    3.1 avoid making calls during the peak-rate period 9 a.m.–1 p.m.

    3.2 prepare for calls before making them to keep time spent on the telephone to a minimum;

    3.3 ring back or leave a message rather than holding on;

    3.4 keep personal calls to a minimum.

4. <u>Personal Calls</u>

    We have never previously attempted to prevent staff making or receiving personal calls — in a small plant like ours there has to be some give and take. I should be grateful, though, if you would ask staff to keep personal calls to a minimum and to use the pay phone in the canteen as far as possible.

    RW

PART

That concludes our look at writing skills.

As we said at the beginning of the unit, learning to write well can be a life's work and is always something which we could improve further.

Nevertheless, I hope the practical hints we have talked about in the unit have been of some use and interest you and that you will feel that bit more confident next time you have to put pen to paper.

If you would like a checklist of points to remember if you are writing a letter, memo, reports or documents for meetings, you'll find these in **Part D, Checklists for Business Writing**.

PART

PART D CHECKLISTS FOR BUSINESS WRITING

1. Introduction

This part of the unit contains four checklists — a brief run-down of points to remember if you are writing letters, memos, reports or the documents which go with meetings.

You may like to refer to them when you are actually writing any of these and you may find it useful to read through them all before you go on to the performance checks in PART E.

2. Letters

● If you are answering a letter which contains a reference, make sure you include the reference on your reply.

● Acknowledge the letter you are answering — 'Thank you for your letter of 8 October . . .'.

● If you know the name of the person you are writing to, use it.

● Give your letter a title if that will make the message easier to understand. The title goes *after* Dear Sir, Dear Mr Smith or whatever.

● Use sub-headings and numbered paragraphs if it will help to make the message easier to understand.

● Plan the letter before you write.

State briefly what the letter is about:

> 'Your North Midlands representative recently suggested that I should contact you about a possible modification to your product line.'

Add to your opening statement if necessary:

> 'We have successfully adapted your standard product to our requirements and feel that many of your customers could benefit . . .'

PART

State your purpose:

'If you feel this modification would be of interest, perhaps you would like to come here to see it in operation.'

Conclusion:

'If the dates I suggest are not convenient, perhaps you would telephone me here and we'll arrange a different time.'

● If you begin 'Dear Sir', finish 'Yours faithfully'. If you begin with the person's name, ('Dear Mrs Smith'), finish 'Yours sincerely', unless your company has a particular house style which is the same on all letters.

● Never have a post-script (PS). If a letter is so badly thought out that you haven't said all you should in the text of the letter, tear it up and start again.

EXTENSION 2
page 90

3.   Memoranda

● We talk about one memorandum (or memo for short) — more than one memoranda or memorandums.

● They are sent instead of letters to people who work in the same company as yourself. You never send a memo to somebody outside the company.

● A memo may be a couple of lines or two pages long but, whatever the length, they all follow the same pattern.

● Most companies have pre-printed memo pads which are either A4 or A5 size. (A4 is the size this unit is printed on, A5 is half that). It usually looks like this.

MEMORANDUM	
From:	To:
Subject:	Date:

PART

- You fill in the details at the top and this means that you don't have any 'Dear Mr' . . . or 'Dear Mike' . . . or 'Yours sincerely' . . . at the end.

- Memos are usually sent to one other person but, if you need to send one to several people then you make this clear when you fill in the top. Like this, for instance:

MEMORANDUM	

From:
    Safety Officer
	To:
	    All Production Personnel

Subject:
    Safety Shoes
	Date:
	    3 Dec

- Like letters and reports, you write memos in complete sentences, not in note form but you keep it as brief as possible.

- As a general rule you only deal with one subject on one memo. If you have two subjects to discuss or comment on, then you send two memos. This is because the memo will have to be filed under its subject, and you can't easily do that if it deals with several topics.

- A memo shouldn't look like a newspaper article.

In order to make your memo as simple to understand as possible you should:

use sub-headings each time you raise a new point;

number each new paragraph.

EXTENSION 3
page 90

4. Reports

- Decide the purpose of the report.

    Is it just to provide information?

    If so to whom and why do they want it?

    or

PART

Are you asked to investigate a problem?

If so, precisely what is the problem and how much authority have you to investigate?

● Decide who is going to read the report.

This will affect how you write it. If it will be read by people in other departments of your company then you will probably have to explain any processes, procedures and technical terms which you use in your own job.

● Check whether there is already a standard form for the report you have to write (e.g. an accident report or dangerous occurrence report form).

● Check whether your company has its own house style for reports (e.g. do they expect recommendations to be at the beginning or the end of the report? Do they expect a separate summary of the report?).

● Collect and organise the material. (Look at page 62 to show you one way of doing this.)

● Write the introduction.

Say what the report is about and why it is necessary. Explain any limiting factors (e.g. shortage of time to investigate further) and any essential background information.

● Under suitable sub-headings and numbering your paragraphs (look at page 68 for a reminder) describe how you set about collecting the information for the report and what you found out.

● Analyse the information you have given and say what conclusions you draw.

● Write the recommendations.

That is, on the basis of the evidence you have given, what you think should be done.

Make recommendations quite specific. A vague recommendation like:

'We should consider trying to reduce waste', is no recommendation at all.

This is a more meaningful recommendation.

'It is recommended that we implement the waste reduction programme described from 1 November with the objective of reducing waste by 40% in the following quarter.'

● Don't introduce any new material or arguments into the recommendations. They should be short and very much to the point.

● Write a summary which briefly says what the report is about and what the main recommendations are. Although you have to write this last, it should appear at the beginning of the report so that your readers can quickly get a grasp of what the report contains.

EXTENSION 4
page 90

● Check the report for mistakes and to make sure that it still meets your original purpose.

PART

● Sign and date it at the end.

5. Meetings

Notice

Before a meeting, however informal, let people have written notice of the

- date

- time

- place

- subject to be discussed

Agenda

The agenda is the list of topics to be discussed. It should be clearly defined well before the meeting.

Here is an example of a formal agenda.

Even if you don't need such a formal document, there are several points worth copying.

AGENDA

1. Apologies for absence

Look around at the beginning. Note who's there *and* who's missing. They'll need to be kept informed.

2. Minutes of the previous meeting

This means that you read out and agree the written record of what happened at the last meeting.

3. Correspondence

4. Cost Saving programme — report

5. New warehouse — revision of schedule

6. Issue of protective clothing to warehouse personnel

7. Any other business

This gives people an opportunity to discuss matters which have arisen too late to be included on the Agenda. It's up to the Chairman to decide how much discussion to allow.

PART

8. Date, time and place of next meeting   If you need to have another meeting, fix the details *now*. If not the group easily runs out of steam. The time between meetings becomes longer and the group loses interest and effectiveness.

Minutes

This is the written record of what took place at the meeting.

- Write notes for the minutes *during* the meeting. (Or, if you are chairing the discussion, ask somebody to do it for you.)

- Write up the minutes within 24 hours of the meeting otherwise you forget what was said.

Here is an extract from some minutes which shows you how they should be set out.

NORTHERN FASHIONSCENE LTD

Minutes of the meeting of the Works Committee held at 9.30 a.m. on Monday 3 December 1984.

Those present: J Harman (Chairman)
                  M Ashford
                  E Jackson
                  D Davies
                  L Simpson
                  J Easby

1. Apologies were received from A Whitehead.

2. The minutes of the Works Committee held on Monday 5 November 1984 were read and approved.

3. *Matters arising*

   M Ashford, Personnel Manager, said that following the last meeting, he had investigated complaints from personnel concerning local bus services and was able to report.

4. *Personnel Manager's report*

   4.1 Following complaints by personnel that they arrived late and had to leave early because of cut-backs in bus services, the United Bus Company had been approached. They confirmed that there was:

   a withdrawal of duplicate buses at peak periods;

   a cut-back in services at peak-load times.

   United Bus Company regretted the situation but felt they could not offer any improvement in the near future.

4.2 Records of staff turnover for the past three years showed a gradually increasing staff turnover rate (3%–7%).

Action Minutes

Here is an example of Action Minutes which are the form of minutes you're likely to find most useful at work. As you see, they mainly record the action to be taken and, in the right hand column, give the initials of the people responsible for taking action.

These are simple and quick to write up and to read and are an effective way of pointing out to people exactly what you want *them* to do before the next meeting.

A BRYSON ENGINEERING

Minutes of the meeting of the Health and Safety Committee held at the Stockbridge plant on 25 February 1984.

Those present: B Williams — Plant Engineer,
C Gaffey — Safety Officer,
S O'Toole — Medical Officer,
H Higgins, S Clarke and A Peters — Health and Safety Representatives.

MINUTES	ACTION TO BE TAKEN BY
1. The emission of fumes from C plant has been totally controlled for the past quarter. B Williams agreed to install a permanent monitoring device to ensure that control continues.	BW
2. C Gaffey reported that new lightweight protective overalls suitable for production areas were now available. Messrs Higgins, Clarke and Peters agreed to organise distribution in A, B and C plants.	HH, SC, AP
3. The committee agreed that the plant needs a permanent full-time nurse rather than the present part-time arrangement. S O'Toole agreed to draft a report for the next meeting on the nursing provision made in other engineering companies of a similar size in the area.	S O'T

PART

PART E PERFORMANCE CHECKS

1. End Checks

Time guide
60 mins You may review your understanding of the unit as a whole by completing this group of questions. DON'T GUESS THE ANSWERS — if you're not sure, flick back into the unit and check before responding.

If you are still unsure then put a question mark against your response before proceeding.

TRUE/FALSE

Respond to each statement by writing TRUE or FALSE in the space provided.

1. People take in facts and figures better if they see them written down. _____

2. If you want somebody's opinion on a very important topic, you should get it in writing. _____

3. You can't do anything about the fact that we all understand something different from every conversation. It's just human nature. _____

4. 'With reference to your letter of . . .' is not a good way of replying to a business letter. _____

5. The simpler your writing is, the better people like it. _____

6. Business letters should be impersonal so the reader understands that what the letter says is on behalf of the whole company. _____

7. Sub-headings and numbered paragraphs are acceptable in business letters. _____

8. We are able to compare figures most easily if they are presented to us in vertical columns. _____

COMPLETION

Complete the following statements with a suitable word or group of words.

9. When you're dealing with people at work, written information is often important _____ to what you say.

10. If everybody in a company receives a memo from the boss at the same time they should feel _____.

11. Instructions which don't have to be carried out immediately should be _____.

12. Everything we write at work either _____ information or _____ information.

13. If you write something, one way to check how easy it is to read is to apply _____.

14. A reading index of 50 would mean the writing was _____ for simple business purposes.

15. In business writing you usually start with the _____ important items and work towards the _____ important.

16. When you write a report you put the sub-headings in _____ writing the text.

MULTIPLE CHOICE

Respond to each question by putting a tick against the ONE answer which is most correct.

17. Writing minutes of a meeting:

   a)   helps to ensure that the decisions reached are carried out;

   b)   encourages people to come to a further meeting;

   c)   means people don't have to come to meetings to find out what's happening;

   d)   means whoever writes the minutes makes the decisions.

18. Giving out written information at the beginning of a discussion means:

   a)   you needn't have wasted everybody's time calling a meeting;

   b)   you make the most efficient use of everybody's time;

   c)   you're not going to allow discussion of any other subject;

   d)   decisions reached are likely to be carried out.

19. You can help sustain the interest of what you write by:

   a)   keeping it as short as possible;

b) writing it in a jokey style;

c) varying sentence length and structure;

d) only using short sentences.

20. Giving what you write a personal touch (saying: 'I'll be glad to discuss this with you further', for instance) means the person you are writing to is more likely to:

a) respond in the way you want;

b) suspect your motives;

c) remember what your letter was about;

d) relate to you on a personal level.

21. Planning the structure of what you write is:

a) important in everything, even filling forms;

b) something you need only do for reports;

c) a good idea if you have time;

d) only necessary if you have very detailed information.

22.

Mrs Elliott agreed to obtain specifications and quotations for a fast tape copier before the next meeting.	CE

This is an extract from:

a) agenda

b) minutes

c) report

d) action minutes

23. Which is the most straightforward and effective of these statements?

a) At this moment in time a large proportion of our technical representatives are graduates.

b) Currently many of our technical representatives are graduates.

c) Many of our technical representatives are currently graduates.

d) Nowadays a large proportion of our technical representatives are graduates.

PART

24. One of these statements is dishonestly written. Which one is it?

a) Five years ago we had an entirely manual system. Now it's largely computerised.

b)   I think our change in the last five years from an entirely manual system to a largely computerised system has enabled the company to survive.

c)   The company's survival is due in part to our change from an entirely manual system to a largely computerised system.

d)   In the last five years we have changed from an entirely manual system to a largely computerised system and it's generally agreed that this improvement has enabled the company to survive.

2.   Tutor Check

Here are two letters.

The first is from a prospective customer, the owner of a hotel in Yorkshire who wants to plant the grounds of the hotel with roses and who is asking for details of what rose trees are available.

The second is from the Customer Service supervisor of A Savage & Son, specialist rose growers. As you see, the letter from A Savage & Son contains some useful information but it isn't very well expressed, or logically arranged, or well presented, so that the customer can quickly grasp what he is being told.

Rewrite the letter from A Savage & Son, using the same information to answer the customer's enquiry but expressing it more simply, logically and helpfully.

PART

HAWKGARTH HOTEL
Exelby, North Yorkshire

A Savage & Son
Reading Road
Binchester
Berkshire
BC2 6QX
4 August 1985

Dear Sir

I read with interest the article 'Roses for all reasons' in Sunday Mail yesterday in which you were mentioned as providing a free advisory service on planting and cultivating roses.

This hotel stands in two acres of grounds which used to be well known in the area for its splendid display of roses. We have several interesting photographs taken before the Second World War which bear this out. However, its requisition during the war as a military establishment, subsequent years of neglect followed by fifteen years use a boarding school means that the former rose gardens have virtually disappeared.

I anticipate that re-stocking the grounds will take about five years and thought in terms of starting this year with hedges, roses amongst the trees in the woodland and climbers in difficult positions which will all take some years to achieve maturity.

I should be interested to know therefore what you would suggest for the following:

1. climbers for a north facing, random stone wall of the main wing of the hotel, approximately 80 feet long;

2. a vigorous tall hedge to screen adjoining farm buildings and to deter animals from the farm from coming through the fence onto our property;

3. ramblers to grow amongst trees on the edge of an existing copse of trees (rather neglected at the moment) in a shaded corner of the grounds. I hoped that planting some roses there would give colour and interest to an otherwise rather dull area.

I look forward to hearing from you.

Yours faithfully

S Hamlin

PART

A Savage & Son
Rose Specialist
Reading Road
BINCHESTER
Berkshire
BC2 6QX

Mr S Hamlin
Hawkgarth Hotel
EXELBY
North Yorkshire

7 August 1985

Dear Sir,

With reference to your letter of 4 August, we shall be delighted to help you re-stock your rose garden and offer the following suggestions. A copy of our catalogue is enclosed so that you can consider the entire stock list for yourself. The ideal planting time for roses is November/December though any time until March is possible provided there is no danger of severe frost. However, I do advise you to place your order as soon as possible so that the roses are despatched in time for autumn planting provided, of course, that you are ready to plant them then. Our roses are packed in peat and polythene and will tolerate being kept in dark, frost-free conditions for up to three weeks prior to planting.

As I said, you may like to choose alternatives from the complete stock list but I suggest the following. Alberic Barbier would do well climbing against a north wall and will also grow into trees satisfactorily, though you would have to be careful that roses were not planted too close to the roots of trees and, of course, no rose will do well in totally shaded conditions. However, I think you would find that the following would achieve the effect you want in adding interest and colour to the copse:

Alberic Barbier;
Dr van Fleet;
Bobbie James;
Pauls Himalayan Must;
Wedding Day.

This would give you a variety of colour and flowering periods and the additional interest of coloured hips in the autumn.

In addition to Alberic Barbier as a climber for a north wall, you might like to try Gloire de Dijon, Golden Showers, May Queen and New Dawn. This will also give you a variety of colour. You are fortunate in having random stone walls against which almost every colour is seen to advantage as opposed to brick, for instance, which never does justice to reds and crimsons. However, against a north facing wall, with limited direct sunlight, I think you will find that lighter yellows, pinks and whites create a more pleasing effect. Incidentally, May Queen also makes a splendid tree.

PART

As for the hedge, I suggest Nevada, Constance Spry and Fruhlings Gold to give you a variety of colour, though, of course, if you feel that one colour would create a more dramatic effect then you could create a hedge of any one of these. Certainly any of them will give you a tall, impenetrable hedge within a few years.

Judging by the indication of size you have given, I estimate that you would need twelve climbers and fifteen to twenty roses to grow into the copse. You don't give an indication of the length of hedge you require but, to provide a dense hedge of this type you could estimate planting one bush every four feet.

Climbers and the roses for the copse are £3.75 each, hedging plants are £2.75 and we give a discount of 10% on orders over £200. There is a standard charge of £4 per order for packing and carriage but this is waived on orders over £50.

We can offer a more detailed advisory service than I have given if you provide more detailed information of dimensions, aspect, soil type etc and, if required, we will also come and visit a customer's premises to discuss special requirements though we have to charge for this service. I enclose a questionnaire which you might like to complete and return if you would like more detailed advice on planting your grounds. This service is free.

I wish you every success with your roses and we look forward to receiving your order.

Yours faithfully

R Harris
Customer Service Supervisor

Enc

3. Work-based Project

Choose what seems to you a fairly limited problem at work to which you can think of a solution. This might be:

a minor change in a clerical system;

a slightly different way of working;

a change of material or materials handling;

a change of storage arrangements;

something to do with the health, safety or welfare of your workteam.

But those are only suggestions. You may well think of something which doesn't come in any of these categories and exactly what you choose will depend on the nature of your job.

Perhaps you will think of a problem which you have solved fairly recently. In that case, use it for this project, but assume that your solution hasn't yet been put into operation.

Don't choose anything too ambitious because, as you know, it's rarely simple to bring about a major change in one work area without affecting the work of a lot of other people.

Having chosen your problem and its solutions, write a memo to your immediate boss describing precisely what the problem is and what you suggest to improve the situation. Remember to provide enough evidence to support your case and write it in a way which is likely to get a favourable response.

Next assume that what you propose has been agreed to and you can make the change.

How would you inform your workteam?

Would you need to back up anything you say in writing? In one or two sentences write down what you would do to make sure that your workteam took notice of the change you were making and remembered it whenever necessary.

Finally, write out *one* of the pieces of written information which you might use to get your workteam to make the change you suggest effectively and efficiently. This might be a memo, or notice or notes for a briefing session but need not necessarily be any of these.

PART

PART F   UNIT REVIEW

1.   Return to Objectives

Having completed your work on this unit let's review how you feel about each of our four opening objectives. I'll repeat them here and add comment.

You should be better able to

● IDENTIFY THE SITUATIONS IN WHICH YOU NEED TO WRITE THINGS DOWN.

There's nothing particularly special about putting things in writing. Speaking and writing can both be equally effective means of communicating with other people and either can be just what is needed in certain circumstances. You wouldn't, for instance, just tell somebody details of a pay rise without giving them some written confirmation of it and you wouldn't ask one of your workteam who seemed depressed and unable to work properly to jot his worries down on a piece of paper. So there's nothing especially superior about writing. It's just that it does have the advantage of allowing people to refer to it later, if they have to remember details of something slightly complicated, or something which is likely to be open to argument or discussion. And, of course, if you are planning something which hasn't yet happened, like a meeting, then details in writing allow other people to plan too, and thus you make more effective use of your own time and theirs.

So if you now feel that writing things down is not just something which you have to do in certain limited circumstances, but is a communication tool which you can use, judging each situation on its merits, whenever you feel that written information will help people remember, or prepare, better than the spoken work alone would do, then you achieved this objective.

Our second objective is:

You should be better able to

● MAKE YOUR WRITING SIMPLE, DIRECT AND ACTIVE.

The days when business writing was expected to sound rather long-winded and full of jargon phrases like: 'I am in receipt of yours of the 3rd inst.', are fortunately over. But it's still a very natural temptation to write in a rather more wordy style than we would use if we were talking to the same person. Yet everybody appreciates a simple, clear (and preferably short) letter, memo, report or whatever it is that we are faced with reading. Writing simply isn't necessarily easy, it involves thinking for yourself rather than using over-worked expressions which other people have used, and deliberately pausing to ask yourself if one word will do instead of three. It isn't something that you become skilled in overnight, not at the end of working through a unit on the subject for that matter! But if you have found the practical hints in this unit of some use and, when you pick up your pen, you now ask yourself: 'Now how would *I* say this', rather than letting the words form themselves, then you have probably achieved this objective.

PART

88

Our third objective is:

You should be better able to

● VARY THE STRUCTURE OF YOUR WRITING TO INCREASE THE READING INTEREST.

Sometimes we can write something, a short report perhaps, which seems clear enough but it still seems rather heavy-handed and monotonous. Sometimes, worse still, it seems clear enough to us but the people it is intended for seem to have trouble reading it. Possibly the trouble is that the structure is rather unvaried and flat or we may have fallen into the trap of writing such long sentences that the sense gets lost. If this seems to be the trouble, it's worth running a reading index check over whatever we've written. Nobody suggests that you are likely to or need to work out the reading index of everything you write but doing it a few times will help you build up an impression of how readable what you write is and will help you to monitor it as you write.

Similarly, if you get into the habit of varying sentence length as a matter of course, a more varied and readable style will probably follow and you will have achieved this objective.

Our final objective is:

You should be better able to

● ORGANISE YOUR WRITING TO MAKE UNDERSTANDING EASIER AND RESPONSE MORE LIKELY.

Simple, clear writing alone isn't always enough to make sure that what you write is readily understood and acted upon.

When we're faced with a page of written information we usually read it at least twice, unless it's very simple — once to get the general drift of what it's about and once to read it in detail.

If you can signpost what your writing is about by appropriate headings, sub-headings and numbered paragraphs which are in a logical order, you speed up and reinforce the reader's understanding. And, since most people who are working are pretty busy, your reader will appreciate your clarity and be more likely to respond.

In addition to that, you improve your chances of getting the response you want if you let the reader know what you want him to do — whether it's to supply some information, come to a meeting, contact you, or whatever.

If you do both these it means you have thought about the purpose of what you're writing and the surest way of achieving it. This may only take a matter of seconds or, if it is quite a lengthy report or letter you are writing, may be the hardest part of the whole task. Either way, if you now find that, before you write something, you pause to consider why you're writing and how to organise it to achieve what you want, then you have achieved this objective.

I hope that the work you have done was enjoyable and useful enough to encourage you to continue your studies.

PART

2. Extensions

EXTENSION 1   Book: *Super Series Unit 304 — Orders and Instructions*

                   Author: NEBSS/NRMC

                   Publisher: Pergamon Open Learning

If you want to know more about organising information specifically for giving instructions you might find this unit helpful.

EXTENSION 2   Book: *Mastering Business Communication*

                   Author: Woolcott L A and Unwin W R

                   Publisher: Macmillan

This book contains several useful chapters of letters, memos, reports and meetings documents.

EXTENSION 3   Book: *The Business of Communicating*

                   Author: Stanton, N

                   Publisher: Pan Breakthrough Series

EXTENSION 4   If you have to tackle writing quite a lengthy report, you might find it useful to look at the following books:

                   Book: *Scientists must write*

                   Author: Barrass R

                   Publisher: Chapman and Hall 1978

                   Book: *So you have to write a technical report*

                   Author: Gray D E

                   Publisher: Information Resources Press, Washington 1970

                   Book: *Effective technical writing and speaking*

                   Author: Turner B T

                   Publisher: Business Book Ltd 1974

EXTENSION 5   If you would like to know more about running meetings and writing meeting documents, you might find it useful to look at the following:

PART

                   Film/Video: *Meetings, Bloody Meetings*

                   Publisher: Video Arts

Book: *Supervisory Management*

Author: Evans, D

Publisher: Holt Business Texts

These extension opportunities can all be taken up via your Resource Centre.

They will either have the materials or will arrange that you have access to the materials. However, it may be more convenient to check out the materials with your personnel or training people at work — they may well give you access. There are other good reasons for approaching your own people, for example they will become aware of your interest and you can involve them in your development.

3. References

REFERENCE 1 Book: *Principles and Practs of Supervisory Management*

Author: Evans, D

Publisher: Holt Business Texts

REFERENCE 2 Film: *Meetings, Bloody Meetings*

Publisher: Video Arts

REFERENCE 3 Book: *The Complete Plain Words*

Author: Gowers, E

Publisher: Pelican paperbacks

This book was originally written in 1948 to improve Civil Service writing. It is still a classic guide to how to write clearly, simply and accurately — and it is entertaining reading. Chapters 5, 6, 7 and 8 are about the choice of simple, familiar and precise words.

REFERENCE 4 Book: *What do you mean 'Communication'?*

Author: Stanton, N

Publisher: Pan Breakthrough Series

In Chapter 13 kinds of sentence structure of differing complexity are explained.

These references can all be taken up via your Support Centre. They will either have the materials or will arrange that you have access to the materials. However, it may be more convenient to check out the materials with your personnel or training people at work — they may well give you access. There are other good reasons for approaching your own people, for example they will become aware of your interest and you can involve them in your development.

If you do wish to make use of these references then don't think that you must read them right through. Just dip into them for a slightly wider treatment of the topic raised by the unit.

PART

NEBSS RECOGNITION

IT IS IMPORTANT TO HAVE YOUR ACHIEVEMENT RECOGNISED

The National Examinations Board for Supervisory Studies (NEBSS) makes nationally recognised awards to supervisory managers who successfully complete its courses. If you study an appropriate selection of approved units in the Super Series and complete the NEBSS assessments successfully you can obtain NEBSS MODULE AWARDS which lead on to the CERTIFICATE IN SUPERVISORY MANAGEMENT. Some 6,500 of these are already awarded annually to students who have been successful on their courses. They come from a wide variety of industries — production, retail, catering, DHSS, Local Government and Police, to name but a few.

WHY NOT REGISTER WITH NEBSS NOW?

All you have to do is complete the registration form in this unit and send it with your registration fee to NEBSS and we will record your details on computer. We will send you your PASSPORT to a NEBSS AWARD and details of the procedure to be followed in order to obtain NEBSS MODULE AWARDS and the full NEBSS CERTIFICATE. We cannot answer queries arising from the Unit, but we can give information about further Units, Support Centres and NEBSS AWARDS.

Please contact: NEBSS OPEN LEARNING,
                   76 Portland Place,
                   LONDON,
                   W1N 4AA

ORGANISATIONS

Organisations concerned with training in any type of industry may use this material to construct their own training courses.

Membership and Professional Bodies may wish to recognise units, or groups of units for fulfilment, or part fulfilment of the educational requirements of their qualifications.

SUPPORT CENTRES

ASHINGTON, NORTHUMBERLAND TECHNICAL COLLEGE (0670) 813248
BALLYMENA TECHNICAL COLLEGE (0266) 2871/4
BATHGATE, WEST LOTHIAN COLLEGE OF FURTHER EDUCATION (0506) 634300
BEDFORD COLLEGE OF HIGHER EDUCATION (0234) 51671
BELFAST, COLLEGE OF TECHNOLOGY (0232) 227244
BIRMINGHAM, HALL GREEN TECHNICAL COLLEGE (021) 778 2311
BOSTON COLLEGE OF FURTHER EDUCATION (0205) 65701
BRADFORD AND ILKLEY COMMUNITY COLLEGE (0274) 753000
BRIDGEND COLLEGE OF TECHNOLOGY (0656) 55588
BRIDGWATER COLLEGE (0278) 55464
BURTON UPON TRENT TECHNICAL COLLEGE (0283) 45401
CANTERBURY COLLEGE OF TECHNOLOGY (0227) 66081
CARDIGAN COLLEGE OF FURTHER EDUCATION (0239) 612032
CARLISLE TECHNICAL COLLEGE (0228) 24464
CASTLEFORD, WAKEFIELD DISTRICT COLLEGE (0977) 554571
CHESTER COLLEGE OF FURTHER EDUCATION (0244) 677677
CLYDEBANK COLLEGE (041) 952 7771
COLCHESTER INSTITUTE (0206) 570271
COSHAM, HIGHBURY COLLEGE OF TECHNOLOGY (0705) 38131
COVENTRY TECHNICAL COLLEGE (0203) 57221
CRAWLEY COLLEGE OF TECHNOLOGY (0293) 512574
CREWE AND ALSAGER COLLEGE OF HIGHER EDUCATION (0270) 583661
CROYDON COLLEGE (01) 688 9271/6
DARLINGTON COLLEGE OF TECHNOLOGY (0325) 467651
DERBYSHIRE COLLEGE OF HIGHER EDUCATION (0332) 47181
DUNDEE COLLEGE OF COMMERCE (0382) 29151
DURHAM, NEW COLLEGE (0385) 62421
EDINBURGH, STEVENSON COLLEGE OF FURTHER EDUCATION (031) 453 6161
ENNISKILLEN, FERMANAGH COLLEGE OF FURTHER EDUCATION (0365) 22431
EPSOM, NORTH EAST SURREY COLLEGE OF TECHNOLOGY (01) 3941731
GATESHEAD TECHNICAL COLLEGE (0632) 4771714
GLASGOW, STOW COLLEGE (041) 332 1786/7/8/9
GLENROTHES AND BUCKHAVEN TECHNICAL COLLEGE (0592) 772233
GRAYS THURROCK, THURROCK TECHNICAL COLLEGE (0375) 71621
GREAT YARMOUTH COLLEGE OF FURTHER EDUCATION (0493) 655261
GUILDFORD COLLEGE OF TECHNOLOGY (0483) 31251
HALIFAX, THE PERCIVAL WHITLEY COLLEGE OF FURTHER EDUCATION (0422) 58221
HAWICK, THE BORDERS COLLEGE OF FURTHER EDUCATION (0450) 74191
HEREFORDSHIRE TECHNICAL COLLEGE (0432) 267311/6
HUDDERSFIELD POLYTECHNIC (0484) 22288
HULL, HUMBERSIDE COLLEGE OF HIGHER EDUCATION (0482) 41451
INVERNESS COLLEGE OF HIGHER AND FURTHER EDUCATION (0463) 236681
LEICESTER, WIGSTON COLLEGE OF FURTHER EDUCATION (0533) 885051
LONDON CORDWAINERS TECHNICAL COLLEGE (01) 9850273/4
LONDON HACKNEY COLLEGE (01) 9858484
LONDON (SOUTH WEST) COLLEGE (01) 677 8141
MACCLESFIELD COLLEGE OF FURTHER EDUCATION (0625) 27744
MANCHESTER (CENTRAL) COLLEGE (061) 831 7791
MANCHESTER (GREATER), TAMESIDE COLLEGE OF TECHNOLOGY (061) 339 8683
MANSFIELD, WEST NOTTINGHAMSHIRE COLLEGE OF FURTHER EDUCATION (0623) 27191
NEWCASTLE COLLEGE OF ARTS AND TECHNOLOGY (091) 273 8866

NEWPORT, ISLE OF WIGHT COLLEGE OF ARTS AND TECHNOLOGY (0983) 526631
NORTHAMPTON, BLACKWOOD HODGE MANAGEMENT CENTRE/NENE COLLEGE (0604) 719531
NORWICH CITY COLLEGE OF FURTHER AND HIGHER EDUCATION (0603) 660011
OXFORD COLLEGE OF FURTHER EDUCATION (0865) 512574
PLYMOUTH COLLEGE OF FURTHER EDUCATION (0752) 264746
PONTYPRIDD, POLYTECHNIC OF WALES (0443) 405133
PRESTON, LANCASHIRE POLYTECHNIC (0772) 22141
REDDITCH COLLEGE (0527) 63607/8/9
ROCHDALE, STATE MILL CENTRE (0706) 527102
SHEFFIELD, STANNINGTON COLLEGE (0742) 341691
SLOUGH COLLEGE OF HIGHER EDUCATION (0753) 34585
SOLIHULL COLLEGE OF TECHNOLOGY (021) 705 6376
SOUTHAMPTON INSTITUTE OF HIGHER EDUCATION (0703) 29381 and 28182
SOUTH SHIELDS, SOUTH TYNESIDE COLLEGE (0632) 560403
ST. HELENS COLLEGE OF TECHNOLOGY (0744) 33766
STOCKTON–BILLINGHAM TECHNICAL COLLEGE (0642) 552101
STOKE-ON-TRENT, CAULDON COLLEGE OF FURTHER EDUCATION (0782) 29561
SUNDERLAND, MONKWEARMOUTH COLLEGE OF FURTHER EDUCATION (0783) 487119
SWINDON COLLEGE (0793) 40131
THURSO TECHNICAL COLLEGE (0847) 66161
WATFORD COLLEGE (0923) 41211/6
WEST ANGLIA TRAINING ASSOCIATION LIMITED (0480) 76690
WEST BROMWICH, SANDWELL COLLEGE OF FURTHER AND HIGHER EDUCATION (021) 5569010
WIGAN COLLEGE OF TECHNOLOGY (0942) 494911
WORCESTER, EVESHAM COLLEGE OF FURTHER EDUCATION (0905) 41151
WORCESTER TECHNICAL COLLEGE (0905) 28383
YORK COLLEGE OF ARTS AND TECHNOLOGY (0904) 704141

This list is correct at the time of publication of the unit. If you do not find a Centre near you, please contact NEBSS for the latest list.

THE SUPER SERIES

PRINCIPLES AND PRACTICE OF SUPERVISION

100 Needs and Rewards
101 Enriching Work
102 Workteams
103 Team Leading
104 Leading Change
105 Organisation Systems
106 Supervising in the System
107 Supervising with Authority
109 Taking Decisions

TECHNICAL ASPECTS OF SUPERVISION

200 Looking at Figures
202 Using Graphs
203 Method Study
204 Easy Statistics
205 Quality Control
207 Controlling Output
208 Value Analysis
209 Quality Circles
210 Computers
211 Stores Control
212 Managing Time
213 Descriptive Statistics
215 Supervisors and Marketing

COMMUNICATION

300 Communicating
301 Speaking Skills
302 Writing Skills
303 Communication Systems
304 Orders and Instructions
305 Project Preparation

ECONOMIC AND FINANCIAL ASPECTS

400 Accounting for Money
401 Control via Budgets
402 Cost Reduction
403 Wage Payment Systems
404 The National Economy
405 Cost Centres

INDUSTRIAL RELATIONS

500 Training Plans
501 Training Sessions
502 Discipline and the Law
504 Health and Safety
505 Industrial Relations in Action
506 Equality at Work
507 Hiring People
508 Supervising and the Law

FORM No. OL/50

76 PORTLAND PLACE
LONDON, W1N 4AA
TELEPHONE: 01-580 3050

REGISTRATION FORM FOR OPEN LEARNING STUDENTS   PLEASE USE CAPITAL LETTERS

SUPPORT CENTRE _____

SURNAME	FORENAMES (Initials are not acceptable)	SEX	AGE	Number of Years in Supervisory capacity — if any	Name of Employer if appropriate	Type of Industry

Address

_____

_____

_____

Signed: _____

Date: _____

I enclose a cheque for £5.00 made payable to NEBSS as Registration fee for a period of 3 years.

Please send me my Passport to a NEBSS Award.

For NEBSS use only				Registration No.		

OPEN LEARNING

This Voucher entitles you to an initial FREE CONSULTATION at any of the Support Centres listed in this Unit.

Make contact with the Open Learning Tutor at the Centre and arrange a convenient time for an appointment

Notes

Notes